At Issue

| Genocide

Other Books in the At Issue Series

Athlete Activism
Food Security
Mob Rule or the Wisdom of the Crowd?
Money Laundering
Nuclear Anxiety
Open Borders
Pandemics and Outbreaks
Sexual Consent
Student Debt
Universal Health Care
Vaccination

At Issue

| Genocide

Barbara Krasner, Book Editor

GREENHAVEN
PUBLISHING

Published in 2021 by Greenhaven Publishing, LLC
353 3rd Avenue, Suite 255, New York, NY 10010

First Edition

Articles in Greenhaven Publishing anthologies are often edited for length to meet page
requirements. In addition, original titles of these works are changed to clearly present
the main thesis and to explicitly indicate the author's opinion. Every effort is made to
ensure that Greenhaven Publishing accurately reflects the original intent of the authors.
Every effort has been made to trace the owners of the copyrighted material.

Cover image: Pavel Chagochkin/Shutterstock.com

Library of Congress Cataloging-in-Publication Data

Names: Krasner, Barbara, editor.
Title: Genocide / Barbara Krasner.
Description: First edition. | New York : Greenhaven Publishing, 2021. |
  Series: At issue | Includes bibliographical references and index. |
  Audience: Grades 9–12.
Identifiers: LCCN 2020000917 | ISBN 9781534507272 (Library Binding) | ISBN
  9781534507265 (Paperback)
Subjects: LCSH: Genocide | Genocide—Case studies.
Classification: LCC HV6322.7 .G445 2021 | DDC 364.15/1—dc23
LC record available at https://lccn.loc.gov/2020000917

Manufactured in the United States of America

Website: http://greenhavenpublishing.com

Contents

Introduction

Beginning in 1933, Polish jurist Raphael Lemkin tried to put a name to the intentional act of killing an entire group of people. He researched history to identify instances of what he eventually called "genocide," stemming from the Greek *genos* ("group") and the Latin *cide* ("killing"). He found that genocides have been taking place since ancient times. The most studied genocide is the Holocaust (1941–1945), the systematic murder of six million European Jews carried out by Nazi Germany and its collaborators. Other groups were targeted for elimination as well, including Roma, Jehovah's Witnesses, gays, Afro-Germans, and the mentally and physically disabled. Anthropologist Alexander Laban Hinton labels the Holocaust as a prototype of genocide.[1] Yet other devastating genocides have also occurred—particularly in the twentieth century—including the Armenian, Cambodian, Rwandan, and Bosnian genocides, among others.

The United Nations adopted the term "genocide" via its Convention on the Prevention and Punishment of the Crime of Genocide in December 1948. This convention defined genocide in legal terms for the purpose of punishment through international law. Key to punishment is proving that accused perpetrators had deliberate intent to commit genocide. Lemkin discusses four targeted identity groups: national, ethnic, racial, and religious.[2] However, some scholars argue that each of these groups is artificially constructed.

Scholars have debated the meaning of genocide since the term's inception. Each academic discipline has sought to define it according to the principles of that discipline—sociology, anthropology, political science, history, psychology, and law. Leading genocide specialists have also proposed frameworks for analyzing and understanding genocide. David Moshman, for example, suggests genocide has four overlapping phases:

dichotomization, dehumanization, destruction, and denial.[3] The process of genocide, he argues, begins with an "us" and a "them"—that is, a delineation of insiders and outsiders. The outsiders become a "question" or a "problem" to be solved through social engineering or cleansing. In other words, people must be eliminated.

Media and other forms of propaganda campaign to dehumanize the outsiders and denounce them as subhuman and not worthy of life. Destruction of these "subhumans" then becomes—in the minds of perpetrators—morally imperative because these perpetrators have come to believe they are the actual victims. Perpetrators target certain groups and genders because their elimination prevents the continuation of that group. Genocide often occurs under the cover of war.

Some scholars contend that colonialism, imperialism, and the rise of nation-states gave rise to genocide. Examples from the nineteenth-century scramble for Africa exemplify this. For instance, Germany established colonies in German South West Africa (1884–1915, which became Namibia after its independence). It created processes for incarcerating the indigenous Herero people and ultimately killing them in the name of white European supremacy. In Rwanda, the Hutus and the Tutsis shared a nationality, ethnicity, race, and religion. What they did not share was power and privilege. The conflict between them stemmed from colonialism, when the Germans and Belgians preferred one group over the other. Germany governed Rwanda—then known as German East Africa—from 1885 to 1919, and Belgium took over control from 1916 to 1945, creating a long legacy of colonialism and ethnic division.

Genocide doesn't occur overnight. There is typically a long brewing period. For instance, prior to the Armenian genocide of 1915, there had been previous attempts in the 1890s by the Turks to eliminate the Armenians. The Turks believed the Armenians stood in the way of their nationalistic rise. In Rwanda, although the genocide occurred in the spring of 1994, its roots took shape in 1959 when a Hutu uprising catalyzed Tutsis to flee the country to save their lives. Destruction may take years or days. In Rwanda, the attacks on the Tutsi lasted merely one hundred days. During the Holocaust, killings took place across several years, between 1939 and 1945.

Many scholars have examined the nature of perpetrators. Holocaust specialists Christopher Browning and Daniel Goldhagen both studied Police Battalion 101—a Nazi police force that operated under the SS—and came to different conclusions. Browning argues that members of the battalion were just ordinary men, driven by social pressure to kill. Goldhagen, on the other hand, maintains that these men wanted to kill.[4] In 1961, philosopher and journalist Hannah Arendt attended the trial of the Nazi Adolf Eichmann in Israel. Eichmann had been a mid-level SS officer and one of the organizers of the "Final Solution," the extermination of European Jews. Arendt wrote an article for the *New Yorker* in which she discussed the "banality of evil" she witnessed in Eichmann.[5] By this she meant that Eichmann presented himself as an ordinary person with little special about him. She argued that ordinary people could become capable of extreme acts of violence, as demonstrated by Eichmann. Arendt's portrait clashed with the idea that genocidal killers were monsters, and her observations became and remain highly controversial.

Denying acts of genocide has also made headline news and created controversy. A key example of denial is the now-infamous libel case of Holocaust denier David Irving against American scholar Deborah Lipstadt, author of the 1994 book *Denying the Holocaust: The Growing Assault on Truth and Memory*, and her publisher. Irving claimed that Lipstadt's work unjustly resulted in public hatred of him. Irving lost the case, as the court found that Lipstadt's claims regarding Irving's distortion of facts about the Holocaust were true.[6] Intrinsic to proving denial claims is the presentation of expert witnesses and education for the public.

Genocide denial can also happen on a national level. Poland issued a law in 2018 outlawing statements claiming that the country collaborated with Nazi Germany in killing Jews. Turkey continues to officially maintain that the Armenian genocide (1914–1923) did not happen, even more than one hundred years after the fact. Serbia does not officially recognize the Bosniak genocide (1995). Continual denial places pressure on the international legal system to prosecute acts of genocide, and it questions the validity of the experiences of the survivors. Genocide scholars, legal experts, and administrators remain unconvinced that the UN Convention holds adequate power, since the International Criminal Court has not been able to effectively prevent or punish genocide. Despite an international legal system, genocide continues into the twenty-first century. We read now about crimes against the Rohingya people in Myanmar and the plight of the Yazidi persecuted by ISIS in Iraq. Continued acts of destruction specifically aimed at selected populations raise questions about the viability of genocide prevention and the effectiveness of the court system. For example, have the trial results of Holocaust, former Yugoslavian, and Rwandan perpetrators satisfactorily punished those responsible and deterred future genocides? Have we really learned any lessons? Can justice be served? Can genocide be prevented and, if so, what are the signs of trouble?

Political scientist Barbara Harff developed an algorithm of more than two hundred variables to quantitatively predict possible genocide conditions, which may enable more effective detection and prevention going forward.[7] Intergovernmental agencies, nongovernmental organizations, and nonprofits monitor world events with an eye toward warning signs. But even if they issue warnings, whose responsibility is it to intervene? Debates continue about the efficacy of the United Nations in this regard.

As the viewpoints in *At Issue: Genocide* illustrate, the debates about the causes, consequences, and prevention of mass killings with the intention of physical, biological, and cultural extermination are global in nature and ongoing between many disciplines. While Raphael Lemkin outlined these myriad causes many decades ago, we sadly continue to watch them play out to this day.

Notes

1. Alexander Laban Hinton, "Critical Genocide Studies," *Genocide Studies and Prevention 7*, no. 1 (2012): 13.

2. As quoted by A. Dirk Moses, "Lemkin, Culture, and the Concept of Genocide," in *The Oxford Handbook of Genocide Studies*, ed. Donald Bloxham and A. Dirk Moses (New York: Oxford University Press, 2010), 23.

3. David Moshman, "Us and Them: Identity and Genocide," *Identity: An International Journal of Theory and Research 7*, no. 2 (2007): 115.

4. Christopher R. Browning, *Ordinary Men: Reserve Police Battalion 101 and the Final Solution in Poland* (New York: HarperPerennial, 2017), 184, and Daniel Jonah Goldhagen, *Hitler's Willing Executioners: Ordinary Germans and the Holocaust* (New York: Random House/Vintage, 1997), 9.

5. Hannah Arendt, "Eichmann in Jerusalem," *New Yorker*, February 8, 1963, accessed January 7, 2020, https://www.newyorker.com/magazine/1963/02/16/eichmann-in-jerusalem-i.

6. Steven Busfield, "Irving Loses Holocaust Libel Case," *Guardian*, April 11, 2000, accessed January 7, 2020, https://www.theguardian.com/books/2000/apr/11/irving.uk

7. Barbara Harff, "A German-born Genocide Scholar," in *Pioneers of Genocide Studies*, eds. Samuel Totten and Steven Leonard Jacobs (New Brunswick, NJ: Transaction, 2002), 108.

1

We Must Commit to the Prevention and Punishment of Genocide

Kyle Matthews and Allan Rock

Kyle Matthews is executive director of the Montreal Institute for Genocide and Human Rights Studies at Concordia University. Allan Rock is president emeritus and a professor of law at the University of Ottawa. He is also the former attorney general of Canada and Canadian ambassador to the United Nations.

Despite the work of Raphael Lemkin and his articulation of genocide, which was adopted by the United Nations Convention of the Prevention and Punishment of the Crime of Genocide in 1948, Kyle Matthews and Allan Rock argue that human rights continue to face serious threats. International criminal courts remain ineffective against the crimes they are assigned to prosecute. Matthews and Rock call for a recommitment to the convention among countries that have yet to adopt these international laws.

This month marks the 70th anniversary of the Convention on the Prevention and Punishment of the Crime of Genocide. This is a foundational piece of international law that was born out of the mass atrocities committed by the Nazi regime against European Jews during the Second World War.

"The World's Disturbing Inaction as the Genocide Convention Turns 70," by Kyle Matthews and Allan Rock, The Conversation, May 31, 2018. https://theconversation.com/ the-worlds-disturbing-inaction-as-the-genocide-convention-turns-70-107783. Licensed under CC BY-ND 4.0 International.

Despite the passage of time, we can still find inspiration in the example of Raphael Lemkin. After fleeing to the United States when he lost his family to the Holocaust, Lemkin campaigned for the establishment of an international law to define and forbid genocide. When his resolution proposing the Genocide Convention was adopted by the United Nations General Assembly in 1948, it became the UN's first human rights treaty.

The Genocide Convention has since led to other norms and mechanisms, two of which are crucial in combating large-scale human rights violations.

The first is the International Criminal Court (ICC), established through the Rome Statute in 1998, with a mandate to prosecute those who commit the crime of genocide. The second is the Responsibility to Protect (R2P), a global political commitment to prevent and interdict genocide and ensure the Convention is operational. R2P was initiated in 2001 under the leadership of Canada, and endorsed by all UN member states in 2005 at the UN World Summit.

Yet the conditions that led to the Genocide Convention hold ominous similarities to our world today. The protection of human rights, the commitment to multi-lateralism and our rules-based international order are all under threat.

'Mute and Dysfunctional'

The ICC is under fierce partisan attack. Nationalism and xenophobia in Europe and Asia have produced authoritarian regimes, emboldened by a White House that has relinquished moral leadership and condones their worst behaviour. And the UN Security Council, responsible for acting on humanity's behalf, stands by mute and dysfunctional.

Most troubling of all, there has been a resurgence of the very crimes the Genocide Convention was intended to address.

In August, a UN fact-finding mission determined the state-led ethnic cleansing of Rohingya Muslims in Myanmar to be an act of genocide. This was echoed one month later by Canada's parliament, which voted historically to recognize the events as genocide, calling for the prosecution of those in the Burmese military who are responsible.

Meanwhile, the Uyghurs are still being rounded up in mass detention camps in western China, facing the prospect of annihilation. And the Yazidis, a minority group in Iraq, endured attempted genocide at the hands of ISIS, a crime that continues to go unpunished. Nadia Murad, a Yazidi survivor who was sold into sexual slavery, was recently awarded the Nobel Peace Prize for using her voice to campaign for the prevention and punishment of genocide.

Our collective response to these heinous crimes has fallen far short of what the Convention requires. Most UN member states have shown reluctance even to use the term "genocide" when it obviously applies, no doubt worried they'll be called upon to meet the responsibilities laid out in the Convention—to prevent and to punish.

Inaction Now the Norm

So inaction in the face of mass atrocity has sadly become the norm. While R2P was adopted relatively recently, it is already in danger of atrophying to irrelevance. R2P has not led to effective responses in Syria, Iraq, Myanmar, Yemen or South Sudan. Indeed, R2P has not been meaningfully invoked since the controversial 2011 intervention in Libya.

While there are ample grounds to criticize the way R2P was implemented in that case, it is shameful to use those concerns as an excuse for doing nothing to prevent atrocities elsewhere. The five permanent members of the UN Security Council must take up their responsibility and stop abusing their undeserved privilege to advance their narrow self-interest.

History shows that individuals like Raphael Lemkin and Nadia Murad can make a difference. But the promise of "never again" will ring hollow in the absence of political leadership.

Only 149 UN member states have ratified the Convention, leaving 45 to do so. Adama Dieng, the UN's special adviser on the prevention of genocide, has launched an appeal for universal ratification.

Faced with a lacklustre response, he said this:

> *What message are those states sending, 70 years after the adoption of the convention? That genocide could never happen within their borders? That is being naïve. History has shown us time and again that genocide can happen anywhere.*

Heeding history's call, we must reaffirm our commitment to the Genocide Convention and work towards universal ratification. More importantly, we must abide by the convention's terms and show the moral courage of our convictions.

The Genocide Convention's anniversary comes at a perilous time. But it can also be a moment of promise if we summon the spirit of 1948 and renew our collective determination to prevent and punish the most serious crime of all.

2

Turkey Must Acknowledge and Remember the Armenian Genocide

*Alexander Hinton, Doga Ulas Eralp, Noëlle
Vahanian, and Ted Bogosian*

Alexander Hinton is director of the Center for the Study of Genocide and Human Rights and a professor in the anthropology and global affairs departments at Rutgers University in Newark, New Jersey. Doga Ulas Eralp is a professorial lecturer at the American University School of International Service in Washington, DC. Noëlle Vahanian is a professor of philosophy at Lebanon Valley College in Pennsylvania. Ted Bogosian is an Emmy Award–winning filmmaker and television producer, noted for his 1988 documentary An Armenian Journey.

Even after more than one hundred years have passed, Turkey continues to deny the perpetration of the Armenian genocide in which at least 1.5 million Armenians perished. Genocide scholars weigh in with their views about the one-hundredth anniversary of the genocide. Alexander Hinton examines the lessons Turkey could learn through acknowledgment, apology, and reparation. Doga Ulas Eralp recognizes the flight of surviving Armenians in their own diaspora and calls for public memorialization in Turkey. Ted Bogosian argues that celebrities can play a role in swaying the Turkish public to finally acknowledge the genocide. Noëlle Vahanian insists that Turkey must recognize what it denies.

"The 100th Anniversary of the Armenian Genocide," by Alexander Hinton, Doga Ulas Eralp, Noëlle Vahanian, and Ted Bogosian, The Conversation, April 24, 2015, https://theconversation.com/the-100th-anniversary-of-the-armenian-genocide-40434. Licensed under CC BY-ND 4.0.

Today, April 24, marks a day of recognition for the deaths of more than 1.5 million Armenians in what Pope Francis characterized as "the first genocide of the 20th Century." As historians and scholars have noted, about two million Armenians lived in the Ottoman Empire in the years before World War One; there were fewer than 400,000 by 1922, the rest systemically killed or dying from starvation and forced relocation. Turkey has long denied that Armenian deaths constituted "genocide," which is defined as "the deliberate killing of a large group of people, especially those of a particular ethnic group or nation." Turkey has insisted the Armenian deaths resulted from violence in a civil conflict. Turkey withdrew its envoy from the Vatican after the pope's remarks about genocide. We asked scholars to examine issues raised by today's anniversary.

What Turkey Might Learn from a History of Acknowledgments, Apology, and Reparations

By Alexander Hinton, Rutgers University-Newark

In 1915, the late Ottoman Empire committed genocide against its Armenian population. Even if this point is still politically charged and sparks the ire of the Turkish government, almost all scholars agree that a genocide took place. Eventually, perhaps within a decade if recent trends continue, the Turkish position will change.

How might this process of recognition unfold?

A first step would be acknowledgment, that is, the Turkish government's acceptance of what occurred. A "thin" acknowledgment would be more passive, perhaps simply the cessation of its active program of domestic and diplomatic denial. Such a shift would allow small non-governmental spaces of dialogue about the genocide, ones that recently have begun to emerge in Turkey, to gain momentum and grow.

A "thicker" acknowledgment would take things further, involving a more formal and official admission about what occurred in 1915. German president Richard von Weizsäcker's recognition of the Holocaust provides an illustration of such a "thick" acknowledgment.

A second step, building on a "thick" acknowledgment, would be an apology. A number of governments have formally apologized for historical genocides (and some have not, including the US, which has not apologized for the genocide committed against Native Americans), although this has sometimes been done in a halting, half-hearted, or qualified manner.

Examples include the apologies of Australia's Kevin Rudd to Australian aboriginals, Germany's Johannes Rau for the Holocaust, and Canada's Stephen Harper for the Aboriginal residential schools.

Apologies are complicated, ideally involving, as psychiatrist Aaron Lazare has argued, proper acknowledgment of who was involved, what happened, how the event breached the moral contract, and what were the impacts and consequences of the violating act.

Another step might involve reparation, an issue that has been a factor in Turkey's denials since there are possibly high financial stakes. But reparations come in many forms. An apology is a sort of symbolic reparation. Alternatively, reparations may involve the return of property or even monetary payments that, while significant, would be acceptable to both Turkey and descendants of Armenian victims.

The road to Turkey's recognition of the Armenian genocide may be long. But as we gaze back at 100 years of denial, it is a good time to look forward to consider the possibilities for acknowledgment, apology, and reparation.

The Effect of 100 Years of Amnesia on the Turkish Population

By Doga Ulas Eralp, American University

The greatest obstacle for Turkey in coming into terms with the humanitarian tragedy of 1915 is not necessarily the recognition of events as genocide but rather the simple but complicated act of collective remembrance.

Following its inception after the collapse of the Ottoman Empire, the Turkish Republic has built its model of new Turkish citizenship around an imposed amnesia of events predating 1923. Accounts of Armenians' sufferings in forced pogroms and violent ethnic cleansing by the Ottoman militia have been conveniently brushed under the carpet, as detailed by University of Massachusetts scholar Rezarta Bilali in "National Narrative and Social Psychological Influences in Turks' Denial of the Mass Killings of Armenians as Genocide," in the Journal of Social Issues.

The areas where historically Armenians have lived in Central and Eastern Anatolia were subjected to a process of Turkification. Properties and wealth confiscated from the Armenians were redistributed between local Kurdish notables and Muslim refugees the Balkans and the Caucasus who were resettled in the vacant Armenian villages.

During the following decades the Ankara Government replaced the old Armenian names of towns and villages with Turkish ones while the now empty churches crumbled and fell into ruins.

Turkish society was forced to confront the issues of 1915 for the first time in the 1970s with the the militant violence of the Armenian Secret Army for the Liberation of Armenia (ASALA) when prominent Turkish diplomats were assassinated as described) by historian Uğur Ümit Üngör.

However, the killings did not induce any cathartic awakening in Turkish collective memory. Turkish government responded by emphasizing the "treasonous" behavior of the Armenian revolutionaries during World War One in the Turkish public education system. The Armenian diaspora responded by launching a global campaign of recognition by 2015.

The diaspora's recognition campaign has been successful as more governments across the globe recognize the events of 1915 as genocide. Yet such global political pressure only serves to make officials in the Turkish government more defiant and further strengthens the hands of Turkish nationalists who frame this campaign as proof of ongoing prejudice against Turkey.

A more fruitful avenue to pursue may be encouraging civil society initiatives that focus on public remembrance and recognition between the Armenian diaspora and Turkey rather than pushing for a political solution to a 100-year old human tragedy.

The Importance of Being Clooney: Can Celebrities Sway Turkish Public Opinion About the Genocide?
By Ted Bogosian, Duke University

Aside from a small, but growing, Turkish intellectual elite—privately educated outside of the country—most Turks either aren't aware of the extent of the Armenian genocide, or aren't able to freely debate it.

It's rarely a part of public conversations: the Turkish government suppresses any form of public acknowledgment of the genocide by designating it a crime under the guise of "denigration of the Turkish nation." (In 2006, a Turkish author was brought to trial for having a fictional character mention the Armenian genocide.)

And Turkey's state-controlled media seems to be doing a good job shaping public opinion. According to a survey from earlier this year, only 9% of Turks want their government to acknowledge the genocide.

Is there any hope for reaching the Turkish public, for raising awareness of atrocities committed 100 years ago?

Enter celebrities. Like it or not, we're in an era of celebrity diplomacy, and the Armenian genocide has become their most recent cause célèbre. Perhaps the 100th anniversary has something to do with it; nonetheless, they've come out in force.

- Last month, George Clooney told journalist Gwen Ifill that "just because the term 'genocide' wasn't coined for 30 more years [after 1915] doesn't mean [the Armenian genocide] didn't happen." On CNN, he argued that the Armenian genocide "needs to be acknowledged" so similar atrocities are never committed again.

- In January, Clooney's wife, Amal—who, according to Time, is "the most famous human rights lawyer in the world"—argued on behalf of Armenia before Europe's top human rights court in a case against a Turkish politician who denied the genocide.
- The web was atwitter earlier this month as the Kardashian clan—including power couple Kim Kardashian and Kanye West—traveled to Armenia, where they visited the Genocide Memorial in Yerevan. During their trip, whenever someone entered "Where is…" on Google, "Armenia" was the first suggestion (meaning it was the most popular search term).
- Meanwhile, actor Hugh Grant and singer Cher have each posted tweets bringing attention to the genocide.

This matters. Celebrities wield extraordinary influence in raising public awareness and swaying public opinion. One recent study showed how Katie Couric's public health campaign on colon cancer screenings had "a substantial impact on public participation in preventive care programs." Another found that young people are more likely to agree with a political position if it's been endorsed by a celebrity.

While the Turkish public may get censored versions of the news on their TVs and in their newspapers, surely some make up a portion of "Kimye's" 45 million Twitter followers.

And where are all the celebrities supporting the Turkish denial, countering the Clooneys and the Kardashians, Grant and Cher?

Virtually nowhere.

Forgetting Is Not the Same as Denying
By Noëlle Vahanian, Lebanon Valley College
Why won't the Armenians forget about the past?

If there is a point that is forgotten, it is that one can only forget what one has acknowledged. In the interest of moving on, Turkey must recognize what it denies. That logic is incontrovertible in spite of so many efforts to take the shortcut to forgetting.

To wit, when Pope Francis called the mass killing of Armenians "the first genocide of the 20th century," Volkan Bozkir, the Turkish minister for European affairs, responded that because the pope is Argentine, and because Argentina housed many Nazis, the Pope could not judge.

For instance, we can read that Turkey is "defined by its divisions, between the secular and the religious, rich and poor, liberal and conservative," and yet that it is united it its refusal to recognize its genocidal past.

We here in the United States have our own issues. President Obama has reportedly declined to use the word "genocide" about the mass deaths in Armenia.

And there's our own history to consider. While the 2009 Native American Apology Resolution recognizes the Federal Government's official depredations of Native Americans, but the word "genocide" does not appear. Instead, the resolution "serves as a settlement of any claim against the United States."

Turkish Prime Minister Ahmet Davutoglu called the European Parliament's resolution to urge Turkey to recognize the genocide "a new reflection of the racism in Europe."

Would Europe be so insistent if the Armenians had not been Christians, but "savage" or "primitive" natives? We only have to look to the case of Native Americans to answer that. But, surely, that does not make the wrong of genocide a right. Nor does it make the Armenian genocide a lie.

If even the Pope is not "innocent," who are we to judge? But recognizing genocide is not about Turkey alone conceding guilt for what happened in the past. It's not about giving a pass to those who benefit from war and conquest. It is about forgetting.

That is also why we remember April 24, 1915.

3

Stalin's Genocide by Famine in Ukraine Deserves Public Recognition

Alec Torres

Alec Torres is currently the National Review Institute William F. Buckley Journalism Fellow, a fellowship presented by the conservative magazine the National Review *to young political journalists.*

Although the Soviet Union was not as efficient in its methods of mass extermination as Nazi Germany, the death toll from Stalin's deliberate starvation of Ukrainians in 1932–1933 was staggering. This genocide by famine—known as the Holodomor—primarily affected Ukraine, the breadbasket of the Soviet Union. The years 2012–2013 marked the Holodomor's eightieth anniversary, yet relatively few people knew about or acknowledged this reign of terror. Alec Torres argues it is high time to publicize the suffering, death, and eventual diaspora that resulted from the Ukrainian genocide.

We went to a field. We had nothing to eat. Everything was taken from us. So my mother decided we would go to the field, find some half-frozen potatoes, some kind of vegetables, to make a soup. At that time the Soviet Union was teaching people to report on each other, to spy on each other. Somebody saw that we came with some vegetables, half-frozen, and they arrested my mother. That was the last time I saw her."

"Ukraine's Genocide by Famine," by Alec Torres, *National Review*, November 9, 2013. Reprinted by permission. © 2019 National Review, Inc.

So Eugenia Dallas, originally Eugenia Sakevych, began her story to me. Born in Ukraine around 1925 (she does not know her exact age), Eugenia lived through the Holodomor—genocide by famine—as a young girl. Shortly before her mother was taken, her father was sent to Siberia, deemed a criminal because he owned a few acres of land.

In 1932–33, Ukraine was brought to its knees. After years of mass arrests and deportations had failed to bring the Ukrainians into line, Stalin decided to crush this proud nation with a new weapon: food. Ukraine, once the breadbasket of Europe, was stripped of its grain. With its borders sealed and its citizens imprisoned, an estimated 4 to 14 million people starved to death as food rotted in silos or was sold abroad. Stalin wanted purity, and Ukraine's nationalism threatened his perverse utopia.

"I would go to the store where the bread was; there were lines of no end, and people standing overnight waiting for a loaf of bread," Eugenia told me of her time living in Kiev during the genocide. "One man came out of the store with a loaf of bread. As he was biting his bread, he dropped dead. He died immediately because bread on an empty stomach is like cement. And many, many people died. Nobody paid attention."

This year marks the 80th anniversary of the Holodomor. In remembrance of this crime, the Center for US-Ukrainian Relations (CUSUR) hosted an academic conference, "Taking Measure of the Holodomor," to try to answer the most basic questions about the genocide. Why? Where? How? Who carried it out? Who suffered? How many suffered?

A surprisingly small amount is known for certain about an event with a death toll that rivals that of the Holocaust. I spoke with Walter Zaryckyj, the coordinator of the conference and executive director of CUSUR, and asked him why answers to such basic questions remain indefinite. In short, he said, the records are spotty and, for a long time, the world press was not interested in bringing the truth to light.

"The Bolsheviks were never as efficient as the Nazis, and therefore evidence of the scope and ultimate meaning of the atrocity committed upon the Ukrainian nation, in contrast to the terror unleashed upon the Jews in Europe, has been harder to cull and identify," Professor Zaryckyj told me. "As a consequence, it has been difficult to provide simple and succinct responses concerning the Holodomor that would allow for the kind of full-throated condemnation that the Holocaust justly receives." Fortunately, archives—notably, formerly classified KGB archives—are finally making their way to the West.

However, the historiography of the Holodomor must overcome not only the relative deficiency of records but also a past of denial and deception. The USSR began its propaganda campaign to convince the world there was no famine before the genocide even ended. As the Ukrainian people starved, the country's grain was gathered and sold to the West, fueling the Soviet industrial machine. The word "famine" itself was banned from use in Ukraine. Though reports of mass starvation leaked out, the West could not believe a food shortage would exist amidst such abundance. In those pre-Holocaust days, Westerners could not believe a regime would strategically murder its people. Journalists, such as the now-infamous Pulitzer Prize winner Walter Duranty of the *New York Times*, told the world, "There is no famine or actual starvation nor is there likely to be." And, as one speaker at the conference put it, the West, "either deceiving or wanting to be deceived," looked away.

Later attempts to bring the Holodomor to public attention were denounced by the Soviets as lies and, at times, even denied coverage by Western media outlets. As Peter Paluch reported in National Review ("Spiking the Ukrainian Famine, Again," April 11, 1986), *Time* and PBS, among others, refused to cover a critically acclaimed documentary on the genocide, *Harvest of Despair*. Though some European papers reported on the Holodomor, "the American media were damningly silent," Paluch wrote, "both about the genocide and about Soviet manipulation of the foreign press." (Because of the lack of coverage, William F. Buckley Jr.

hosted a special session of *Firing Line* on which he showed the documentary in full.)

Though the most basic questions haven't been definitively answered, the legacy of the Holodomor lives on. "We always heard about the genocide; now we understand that with the genocide we had an additional component called 'ethnic cleansing,'" Zaryckyj told me in reference to the Soviet efforts to Russify Ukraine through reeducation, deportation, and immigration. "The long-term cultural and political consequences are to break the back of the Ukrainian nation in eastern Ukraine."

Caught between East and West, Ukraine today is faced with the same choice as the other nations that were in the Soviet bloc. Will it be pulled back into Russia's orbit or join the world of the democratic West? "Right after the famine, we discovered that the population of non-Ukrainians in Ukraine went from 7 or 9 percent to 21 or 22 percent," Zaryckyj said. These non-Ukrainians, along with the Russified Ukrainians, "continue to vote, or did until recently, even after the collapse of the Soviet Union."

Putin's Russia has made little effort to hide its imperialistic ambitions, expanding its influence in Georgia, Syria, and beyond. Ukraine's choice—whether to turn back to Russia or integrate into the West—will undoubtedly influence power dynamics throughout Eastern Europe and potentially greater Eurasia.

"We're running against a time limit," Zaryckyj told me. "This is the 80th anniversary, so even the youngest—the eight-year-olds and seven-year-olds who saw it and lived—are now 87 or 88. So there is a definite urgency to get the story out as quickly as possible."

The event ended with a reception remembering those who died in the Holodomor and honoring those who survived. Students from the Ukrainian Student Association of America read the testimonies of several survivors, five of whom were in attendance and were publicly recognized, as well as the names of all those who perished in a very small, unnamed village. As the room sat in silence, the reading continued for over ten minutes.

Speaking with Eugenia, I asked her what it's like to look back on the Holodomor as one of the last survivors and whether she can ever forgive the Russians for their crimes. At the mention of the Russians, Eugenia spoke more quickly, her brow suddenly furrowed. "They destroyed my life, they destroyed my family, they destroyed my country. My family was a good example of what they did with Ukraine. They're bandits, I call them. And not one brought to justice. Look at the Germans; all were brought to justice. But for Ukraine, nobody."

Outside of this brief moment, Eugenia was nonetheless upbeat.

She expressed great pride in Ukraine and told me that she thinks she lived in order to bring its message to the world. She is a public speaker on the Holodomor, has written an autobiography titled *One Woman, Five Lives, Five Countries* with a complementary documentary, and hopes to produce a film soon.

After her mother's arrest, Eugenia was initially sent from Ukraine to a Nazi work camp and eventually fled to Italy; she has now settled in Los Angeles. "I am very happy that I came to the United States," she told me. "Freedom for me is a joy. It's a blessing. We have problems here, but they're minor. People still live well. They're free mentally. In Ukraine, they lived in open prisons under the Soviets."

As other guests shuffled around us, anxious to speak with Eugenia themselves and hear her story in person, she pulled out a copy of her book and read to me one of her poems, called "My Childhood."

Why was my life spared? . . .
Ukraine by evil force was occupied.
Million souls were crucified,
The rest conveniently Russified.
My parents were arrested,
Their identity stripped.
Why was their destiny so cruel?
Today I ask for what reason were they punished?

4

The Time to Remember the Holocaust Is Also the Time to Act

Mark L. Schneider

Mark L. Schneider is a senior adviser in the Americas Program and Human Rights Initiative at the Center for Strategic and International Studies, which is headquartered in Washington, DC.

Each spring there is a Week of Remembrance of the Holocaust, starting with Yom HaShoah—the day of the Shoah, or the Holocaust. Mark L. Schneider argues that at the time of remembrance, the international community should not only pay homage to the victims of the Holocaust but also take action for the prevention of genocide. He calls attention to the UN's "Responsibility to Protect" doctrine from 2005 as a reminder of the international community's obligations.

Today is Yom HaShoah, the start of the Week of Remembrance of the Holocaust. It also should be a time of clarity and commitment to do all in our power to prevent a recurrence of that horrific evil and other crimes against humanity. Each year at this time, I recall my visits to the Terezin concentration camp, to Yad Vashem in Israel, and to the US Holocaust Museum's powerful exhibits of the gas chambers and the Nazi genocide that killed 6,000,000 Jews during its reign of terror.

"Yom HaShoah: Remembering the Holocaust and Preventing Future Genocides," by Mark L. Schneider, Senior Advisor (non-resident), Americas Program and Human Rights Initiative, Center for Strategic and International Studies, April 24, 2017. Reprinted by permission.

A few years ago, I saw the movie *In the Land of Blood and Honey* at the Holocaust Museum. The movie was about Bosnia in the 1990s. It depicted a woman being raped—as more than 20,000 Bosniak women are estimated to have been raped as an instrument of war in that conflict. It showed a child murdered and unarmed men and boys lined up, shot, and their bodies bulldozed into a mass grave.

Despite the demand "never again" after the Holocaust, in places like Bosnia and Rwanda in the early 1990s, in Darfur in the last decade, in the Central African Republic, innocent men, women, and children have been the victims of mass murder. In Syria alone, some 470,000 have been killed since 2011. South Sudan's internal conflict in the past few years has seen more than 50,000 dead and 1.6 million displaced. There have been rampant rapes of Nuer and Dinka women as their towns were overrun by competing forces. As a result of the violence and conflict in South Sudan, Somalia, Nigeria, and Yemen, an estimated 20 million men, women, and children are facing famine.

The Days of Remembrance are a time to focus on how the United States and the international community can do more than lament and condemn mass atrocities and crimes against humanity. Yes, it is a time to remember the extreme nature of anti-Semitism and the Nazi doctrine that denied the humanity of Jews. It also is a time to rededicate ourselves to ending genocide, ethnic cleansing, war crimes, and crimes against humanity against any specific group of human beings.

There have been attempts to establish early warning systems to identify atrocities before they occur and to collectively demand responses. But we have yet to achieve the kind of effective, long-term approach that puts genocide and mass atrocity prevention at the top of our national security agenda. And that is even with the assertions by the Obama administration in 2011 that preventing mass atrocities and genocide is a "core national security interest and a core moral responsibility of the United States." The Atrocity Prevention Board established at the time has worked to pull together an interagency focus on early warning triggers. However, the link between warning and response too often has been missing.

An attempt at the international level was the adoption by the UN General Assembly of the "Responsibility to Protect" doctrine at the World Summit in 2005. It came after a remarkable civil society coalition across the globe came together to press for its approval. It aimed at assuring that national sovereignty could never again justify ignoring when governments failed to act, were unable to act, or were complicit in the face of genocide, ethnic cleansing, war crimes, and crimes against humanity.

The Responsibility to Protect has three foundational pillars:

- Pillar One confirms that the primary responsibility lies with the state to protect its own citizens from genocide, war crimes, ethnic cleansing, and crimes against humanity;
- Pillar Two affirms the international community's responsibility to assist states in building critical capacities to protect their populations and addressing drivers and triggers before the commission of mass atrocity crimes;
- Finally, Pillar Three asserts that the international community has the responsibility to take timely and decisive action using appropriate diplomatic, humanitarian, and other means to prevent and halt genocide, ethnic cleansing, war crimes, and crimes against humanity when a state is manifestly failing to protect its population. This obligation may be even more critical today—when ISIS and other violent nonstate actors are carrying out the atrocities.

The Responsibility to Protect doctrine has been cited multiple times by the Security Council when there was a consensus for collective military and noncoercive action to halt ethnic or other atrocities. And there have been some successes. But where other competing interests intervened, as in Syria, Yemen, or South Sudan, the responses have fallen short and the list of victims continues to grow. And too often when there has been intervention, the responsibility to rebuild after the intervention—as in Libya—has been absent or inadequate. In this environment, there is an urgent need to rethink and revitalize the Responsibility to Protect doctrine to deal with a wide range of threats from state and nonstate actors.

Yom HaShoah is a time to remember. It also is a time to act.

5

Intent to Destroy Must Be Proven in the Genocide Case Against Myanmar

Mauro Barelli

Mauro Barelli is a senior lecturer in law at the City Law School of the University of London. He previously taught at the University of Cardiff in Wales. His work focuses on the rights of ethno-cultural groups, particularly indigenous peoples.

Key to proving that an act of genocide has been committed is showing a specific intent to destroy a national, ethnic, racial, or religious group either wholly or in part, as articulated in the UN Convention of 1948. In 2019, Myanmar's political leader Aung San Suu Kyi had to travel to The Hague's International Court of Justice (ICJ) in the Netherlands to face allegations of genocide perpetrated against Rohingya Muslims. Mauro Barelli asserts that the ICJ's previous rulings have not found states responsible and that it will take years for the court to come to some conclusion about Myanmar.

In what is likely to be a remarkable moment for international justice, Aung San Suu Kyi, the political leader of Myanmar and a Nobel peace prize winner, will be in The Hague this week to lead her country's defence against allegations of genocide.

On November 11, the Gambia launched proceedings against Myanmar before the International Court of Justice (ICJ) for alleged violations of the Convention on the Prevention and Punishment of the Crime of Genocide. I have looked into the question of atrocity crimes, including genocide, as part of my recent research on the principle of the responsibility to protect in international law.

The case focuses on the clearance operations carried out from around October 2016 by Myanmar's military and security forces against the Rohingya Muslims, a distinct ethnic and religious group that resides primarily in Myanmar's Rakhine state.

The Gambia claims that those operations amounted to a genocidal campaign of violence that included mass murder, forcible displacement, rape, and other forms of sexual violence. The UN says that 742,000 Rohingya have fled Myanmar for neighbouring Bangladesh since 2017 and many are still living in dire conditions in refugee camps.

During the public hearings that the ICJ will hold between December 10 and 12, the Gambia will essentially ask the court to order Myanmar to prevent ongoing atrocities against the Rohingya so as to protect them from further, irreparable harm—something known as "provisional measures."

This is the third time that the world's court has been called to establish whether a state is responsible under international law for breaches of the genocide convention. In 2015, the ICJ ruled that neither Croatia nor Serbia had committed genocide during the hostilities that took place in Croatia between 1991 and 1995. In a 2007 case brought by Bosnia-Herzegovina, the court also cleared Serbia of direct responsibility for genocide and complicity in genocide in relation to the 1995 massacre of Srebrenica.

This means that the ICJ has never held a state responsible for committing genocide. In this respect, the 2007 and 2015 verdicts reveal some of the obstacles that the Gambia will face in persuading the court that Myanmar committed genocide against members of the Rohingya group.

Proving 'Intent'

The genocide convention lists a number of acts, including killing or causing serious bodily or mental harm, that may constitute genocide provided that they are committed with the "intent to destroy," in whole or in part, a national, ethnic, racial or religious group.

It is precisely the existence of this special intent that distinguishes genocide from other heinous crimes. This is of special importance given the difficulty of proving genocidal intent in a courtroom. In the absence of direct conclusive evidence, the ICJ will infer genocidal intent from particular circumstances—such as a pattern of acts committed against members of the targeted group—only if the circumstances point unequivocally to the existence of that intent.

Adopting this strict approach in both the 2007 and 2015 judgements, the court determined—with the only exception of Srebrenica—that the atrocities committed during the conflicts in Croatia and Bosnia lacked the requisite intent to destroy the targeted groups, and so could not be qualified as genocide. In the case of Srebrenica, the court ruled that the acts "were committed with the specific intent to destroy in part the group of the Muslims of Bosnia and Herzegovina" and were therefore genocide.

Still, it found that Serbia itself was not directly responsible for the massacre, which was committed by Bosnian Serbs. Serbia was nevertheless found responsible for failing to prevent genocide given that it was in a position of influence over those who devised and implemented it.

The rationale for setting such a high standard of proof is, in the ICJ's words, that: "Claims against a state involving charges of exceptional gravity must be proved by evidence that is fully conclusive."

Unsurprisingly, this stringent approach has been the object of much criticism. One of the current judges sitting at the ICJ, Cançado Trindade, noted in 2015 that imposing such a high threshold for proof of genocide runs the risk of reducing the genocide convention to a dead letter.

UN Fact-Finding Mission

To demonstrate the genocidal nature of the violence against the Rohingya, the Gambia—which is backed by the 57 members of the Organisation of Islamic Cooperation—will rely extensively on UN sources. In March 2017 the UN Human Rights Council created an Independent International Fact-finding Mission on Myanmar and tasked it with establishing the facts and circumstances of the human rights violations committed by Myanmar's military and security forces against the Rohingya.

The implications of the mission's investigative activities could be profound. In the 2007 genocide case, the ICJ relied heavily on the judgements of the International Criminal Tribunal for the former Yugoslavia (ICTY) to conclude that genocide was committed at Srebrenica. The authoritativeness of the UN's factfinding mission to Myanmar cannot be equated to that of a tribunal such as the ICTY. Yet, the ICJ is likely to give serious consideration to the mission's reports in light of the care taken in preparing them, their comprehensiveness, and the independence of those responsible for their preparation.

Crucially, the 2018 and 2019 reports infer genocidal intent behind the attacks against the Rohingya from a number of factors and circumstances linked to, among other others, the brutality and the scale of destruction of the military operations as well as the widespread use of rape and sexual assault during those operations.

The ICJ judges will need to be satisfied with the solidity of this inference of genocidal intent by the UN mission. However, the very fact that they will have to engage with and determine the weight of those findings as evidence will be of paramount importance.

After ruling on the question of provisional measures—and assuming that no jurisdictional obstacles will be identified—

the court will fix time limits for the filing of the parties' written pleadings in the case. After the written and then oral proceedings, the court will begin its deliberation and so it will be some years before a final decision on this important case is made.

6

Lessons to Avoid Another Darfur Genocide

Dwayne Wong

Dwayne Wong is a Guyanese-born author who has written several books on Africa and African diaspora history.

The colonial British governance in Sudan (1899–1956) resulted in different paces of development between the northern and southern regions, which created cultural and ethnic dichotomies. The south went largely ignored. After decolonization, Sudan's south became marginalized and several civil wars broke out. The civil war between the Darfur region and the Sudanese government led to genocide. Farida Nabourema argues that South Sudan's civil war offers lessons about methods for inducing effective change across Africa. One of these lessons is that the creation of a new nation-state is a viable and preferable solution compared to the extreme violence of dictators.

The ongoing civil war in South Sudan offers important lessons about effective and ineffective ways to produce a change in Africa. The conflict that caused the separation between Sudan and South Sudan is one that traces its roots to the European and Arabic conquests of Sudan. Sudan's name is itself a reflection of these foreign conquests because the name Sudan comes from the Arabic phrase "bilad al-sudan," which means "land of the blacks" in Arabic. Africans in the Sudan put up fierce resistance against the Islamic invasions, but over time those in the north adopted the

"Lessons from South Sudan's Civil War," by Dwayne Wong, Africans Rising For Justice, Peace and Dignity, September 10, 2018. https://www.africans-rising.org/lessons-from-south-sudans-civil-war/. Licensed under CC BY-SA 4.0 International.

Arabic religion and culture of the invaders. The southern portion of Sudan continued to practice their traditional religious beliefs, as well as Christianity. British colonial rule helped to further entrench the ethnic and cultural differences between those in the north and those in the south so that by the time Sudan became independent there was a clear distinction between the "Arab" north and the "Black African" south.

During the colonial period, the British developed the north and south very differently. The north received more attention from the British administration, whereas the south was neglected. Darfur, which is located in the north, was also neglected by the British administration. The result of this was that the people of Darfur were excluded from the Arabic ruling class in the north after Sudan became independent. When Sudan became independent the nation was dominated primarily by the Arabised elite in the north. The northern elites have marginalised those in the south and have even tried to impose their Arab identity on the rest of the nation. This led to two separate civil wars between the northern government and rebels in the south. The second of these civil wars resulted in South Sudan becoming a separate nation of its own. There was also a civil war between Darfur and the Sudanese government as well, which has resulted in genocide and widespread rape in Darfur.

There are many examples of opposition groups in Africa that have turned to armed rebellion to oppose oppressive governments. The problem with this form of resistance is that these rebel groups often behave just as badly as the governments that they oppose.

The rebels in the South were no different. The Sudan People's Liberation Army (SPLA), which was led by John Garang from the beginning of the war in 1983 until his death in 2005, was the largest and most powerful of the southern rebel groups that fought against the Sudanese government. Under Garang the SPLA became a very autocratic military organisation and one which frequently targeted civilians. Dr. Peter Nyaba, who was a former military officer with the SPLA, stated:

The SPLA training camps themselves resembled concentration camps in which the recruits and prospective SPLA soldiers are brutalised, dehumanised and de-revolutionised. It was here that the SPLA officers and men internalised oppression and brutality. Once they were deployed at the war front, their first victims became civilians, whom they now terrorised, brutalised, raped, murdered and dehumanised.

Any group that feels it is necessary to take up arms to end oppression has to be cautious about the potential of becoming as brutal as or even more brutal than the oppressive forces that they are fighting against. They also have to be cautious of the fact that violence is not something that can be easily turned off like a switch. Armed conflicts can create a pervasive cycle of violence, which is precisely what we are seeing right now in South Sudan.

The main victims of South Sudan's civil war are civilians, who have endured being tortured, raped, and murdered by the armed combatants. Since the civil war began in 2013, an estimated 300,000 people have been killed. Millions more have been displaced.

The atrocities being inflicted on civilians during South Sudan's civil war is a continuation of the violence that was being carried out by the SPLA and other southern rebel groups during the war against the Sudanese government.

The other issue with such intense violence is that it creates divisions, especially in countries which are as ethnically diverse as South Sudan is. Garang envisioned a "New Sudan" in which the Sudanese national identity transcended tribal and religious affiliations, but Garang was himself guilty of fostering tribalism within his own organisation. Garang was from the Dinka people and his faction of the SPLA was dominated primarily by people from his own ethnic group. In 1991 a splinter faction emerged within the SPLA. The new group, the SPLA-Nasir, not only took issue with Garang's dictatorial leadership methods, but they also espoused secession from Sudan rather than Garang's vision of building a new Sudan. Garang's SPLA was supported by the

Dinka people, whereas the SPLA-Nasir enjoyed the support of other ethnic groups, especially the Nuer. Another organisation that was formed in 1991 was the Nuer White Army. The Nuer White Army and SPLA-Nasir were responsible for massacring 2,000 Dinka civilians in 1991.

Not only was there a civil war between the government in the north and rebel groups in the south, but there was also a civil war between the southern rebel groups. The conflict among the southern rebels did not simply vanish when South Sudan became independent from Sudan. Salva Kiir, who is the current president of South Sudan, became the leader of the SPLA after Garang died. Riek Machar, who is the former vice president of South Sudan and the main rebel leader, was a former member of SPLA-Nasir. The same political and ethnic divisions that arose in the south during the Second Sudanese Civil War were never resolved and the failure to resolve these issues is the reason why South Sudan has been plunged into a civil war.

South Sudan also provides an example of why secession alone is not a solution. Secession seemed to offer an easy solution to the south's problem, but it failed to solve the problems that were really at the root of the crisis in Sudan. As flawed as some of his methods were, Garang's vision for a unified Sudan was the correct vision for resolving the crisis. He envisioned a national Sudanese identity which transcended tribalism. The issue in the Sudan was not that the "Black African" south needed to be liberated from the "Arab" north. Those distinctions were the product of European and Arab imperialism in the Sudan. The issue was the lasting impact of foreign imperialism in Sudan and the only way to correct this issue is to create a new national identity. Garang's vision is even more relevant now given that the role that tribalism has played in South Sudan's civil war.

The other problem is the issue of governance. The rebels in the south were fighting against a theocratic dictatorship in the north which was led by Omar al-Bashir, who has ruled the Sudan since he came to power in a military coup in 1989. Rather than building a democratic and decentralised resistance movement, the SPLA was a dictatorial organisation. Southerners hoped that Salva Kiir would be less dictatorial than his predecessor, but that has not been the case. Kiir engaged in repressive tactics to maintain his tight grip on power, which has included openly threatening journalists and sacking public officials who have been critical of him. Despite the fact that government forces have committed a number of atrocities during the civil war Kiir insists that he is not at fault.

Using extreme violence against the opposition and exploiting ethnic division are two of the main tactics which African dictators have used to maintain themselves in power. These are tactics that Omar al-Bashir has certainly used to maintain his rule on Sudan. The tragic civil war in South Sudan only demonstrates that you cannot effectively combat a dictator by using the same tactics which that dictator uses. The rebels in Sudan tried this and the people of South Sudan are suffering the consequences because of it.

7

American Involvement Is Critical to Genocide Prevention

Nadia Rubaii and Max Pensky

Nadia Rubaii and Max Pensky are codirectors of the Institute for Genocide and Mass Atrocity Prevention at Binghamton University, State University of New York, where Rubaii is an associate professor of public administration and Pensky is a professor in the department of philosophy.

Although genocide prevention is decidedly an international responsibility, the United States is a critical voice in policy and action. However, the American commitment to peacekeeping is lacking in intensity due to the narrow definition of its interests. Nadia Rubaii and Max Pensky argue that budget cuts in the US State Department's Office of Global Criminal Justice will narrow American interests even more severely and limit the effectiveness of international justice to punish genocidal perpetrators.

There are many indications that human rights and international justice are not priorities for President Donald Trump's administration.

As Foreign Policy has reported, one of the likely victims of Secretary of State Rex Tillerson's reorganization and cuts at the State Department is the Office of Global Criminal Justice.

"Are State Department Cuts a Major Setback for Genocide Prevention?" by Nadia Rubaii and Max Pensky, The Conversation, July 31, 2017, https://theconversation.com/are-state-department-cuts-a-major-setback-for-genocide-prevention-81590. Licensed under CC BY-ND 4.0.

This is the office that would, in theory, advise him and other government officials on how the US should act to prevent or respond to genocide, war crimes and crimes against humanity. Given the number of recent, ongoing and potential mass atrocities around the world, some are portraying the decision to shutter the office as a threat to America's moral authority in the field of genocide prevention.

But is that an accurate assessment?

As co-directors of Binghamton University's Institute for Genocide and Mass Atrocity Prevention, we study the causes and consequences of genocides, and what is needed to prevent them. While we agree that US commitment to preventing mass atrocities is important, we argue that the US has for some time been taking more of a back seat on this issue than people realize.

Twenty Years of Small Successes

The Office of Global Criminal Justice was created by Secretary of State Madeleine Albright in 1997 "to focus American foreign policy on preventing and ensuring accountability for atrocities around the world." This was in response to America's failure to act in the face of a preventable genocide in Rwanda in 1994.

Until recently, the Office of Global Criminal Justice was headed by an ambassador-at-large, a diplomat of the highest rank authorized to represent the US internationally. This gave the agency independence and flexibility.

For more than 20 years and under the direction of three ambassadors, the Office of Global Criminal Justice worked with a modest staff of about 12, and an annual operating budget of around US$3 million. That is enough to cover the operating costs of one US aircraft carrier group for about a half a day. Even so, the office helped support the US claim to leadership in battling the worst and most shocking of the world's mass atrocities.

The office has had a number of important wins. It coordinated US policy toward the International Criminal Court and led efforts to provide logistical and financial support to other international tribunals. It established a War Crimes Rewards Program for information leading to the arrest of those wanted in connection with international crimes. It led a campaign to pressure states not to make formal invitations to Sudan's President Omar al-Bashir, an indicted war criminal.

More recently, the office was at the center of efforts to retrieve and authenticate smuggled photographs of victims of the Syrian regime. These photographs also allowed for an unprecedented criminal trial in Spain against the Syrian security forces on behalf of one of the victims. The office has also helped with efforts to declare the Islamic State's violent attacks on the Yazidis in Iraq a genocide.

While important, these actions do not reflect the full potential of the office or the US government in genocide prevention. In our view, the US has very little moral authority to lose if the office is eliminated.

More Talk than Action

The Holocaust is the most widely known example of genocide, war crimes and crimes against humanity. World leaders, including several US presidents, have espoused a commitment to "never again" allow such atrocity. Yet we have seen and continue to see examples, such as recent cases in Bosnia, Rwanda, Kosovo and Darfur, and ongoing situations in Syria and Myanmar, to name just a few. As journalist David Rieff aptly wrote, "never again" has seemed to signify only a US commitment that "never again would Germans kill Jews in Europe in the 1940s."

Genocide prevention requires a global commitment to the value of human lives—even the lives of people who do not live in places with strategic value. But government policies, the US included, often calculate the value of human life based on economic and military measures.

The US has repeatedly defined its interests narrowly—the domestic economy and direct threats to national security. The bar is set very high for the US to commit troops to U.N. peacekeeping efforts. Such conditions almost never exist. The most recent month for which data are available, June 2017, is typical. During that month the US contributed 74 individuals of 96,853 troops, police, military experts and support staff to the United Nations's 15 current peacekeeping operations, none of whom are troops.

Further, the US took nearly four decades to ratify the United Nations Convention on the Prevention and Punishment of Genocide. The convention, which was passed in 1948 and went into effect in 1951, was ratified by 132 countries before the US signed on in 1988. The other 16 stragglers who signed much later were mostly newly formed states, such as former Soviet Republics.

The history of the Office of Global Criminal Justice shows that well-meaning rhetoric often serves to mask lukewarm commitments.

After its inception during the Clinton years, the office survived the George W. Bush administration's unfriendliness to international criminal law.

The office might have expected a friendlier Obama administration. After all, Obama famously declared in 2011 that preventing genocides and mass atrocities would be "a core national security interest and a core moral responsibility" of the American government.

Although the Obama administration did not close the Office of Global Criminal Justice, it did take actions that reduced its effectiveness. When Ambassador-at-Large Stephen Rapp stepped down in 2015, President Obama did not nominate a successor. Todd Buchwald, who currently directs the office, does not have the diplomatic credentials of his predecessors that had been the office's signature.

One could argue that Obama's inattention to the office was offset by his creation of the Atrocities Prevention Board. The board links 11 federal agencies to develop diplomatic, technological, military, educational and other mechanisms for understanding and countering the root causes of genocide.

Yet, while the board opened with much fanfare in 2012, it has since been roundly criticized for secrecy, invisibility and inaction in the face of the unfolding catastrophe in Syria. Along with the Office of Global Criminal Justice, the board too may be soon be dismantled.

Given these shortcomings on genocide prevention, the impact of Trump-Tillerson decisions to eliminate agencies may not be as significant as some expect. But it still sends a very powerful message to the world about the Trump administration's lack of support for global efforts to end impunity.

As Clint Williamson, the Office of Global Criminal Justice's second ambassador, put it recently: "What worries me with this administration is that I am not sure that anyone even supports the very idea of international justice."

That would be good news to current and potential perpetrators of the worst international crimes.

What Comes Next?

By its very nature, genocide prevention is an international effort. An increasing number of nongovernmental organizations in the US and around the world are engaged in prevention efforts. The Auschwitz Institute for Peace and Reconciliation, Genocide Watch, the International Center for Transitional Justice and the Sentinel Project are just a few examples.

Other governments are also stepping up. Lacking the economic or military might of the US, they are working collaboratively and focusing their attention closer to home. Regional associations of government officials dedicated to genocide prevention have formed in Latin America and in the Great Lakes Region of Africa.

Preventing or ending mass atrocities is not a responsibility exclusive to the US, nor is it assured with US leadership. But it is hard to imagine effective prevention without substantial US involvement. Any reductions in US commitment, including the cuts likely under the Trump administration, are cause for concern.

8

Life Force Atrocities Are Early Indicators of Genocide

Elisa von Joeden-Forgey

Elisa von Joeden-Forgey is the Dr. Marsha Raticoff Grossman Associate Professor of Holocaust and Genocide Studies at Stockton University in New Jersey.

Using examples from a variety of genocides, Elisa von Joeden-Forgey argues in this excerpted viewpoint that genocidal perpetrators deliberately commit "life force atrocities," which are intended to destroy both the physical life of members of the targeted group and its sense of community and tradition. For instance, a husband may be forced to watch his wife or daughter sexually violated, knowing that he can never recover from witnessing this act of atrocity. Life force atrocities are ritualized, gender-based acts of violence that are intended to break down the family unit as a source of strength. Von Joeden-Forgey also contends that life force atrocities can serve as early warning signs of genocide.

O ur family tree was obliterated by the genocide. That's where our family begins." This is how Art Tonoyan, a graduate student of religious studies and grandson of survivors of the Armenian genocide, described the genocide's impact on his family. Speaking to the Waco Tribune-Herald in 2005, he told of how his

"The Devil in the Details: 'Life Force Atrocities' and the Assault on the Family in Times of Conflict," by Elisa von Joeden-Forgey, International Association of Genocide Scholars, 2010. Reprinted by permission.

grandfather and grandmother were orphaned by the genocide. His grandmother was too young to remember the details of her orphaning; his grandfather, as a little boy of eight, was forced to watch as Turkish soldiers raped, tortured, and killed his parents and siblings in front of him. The soldiers told him that they would leave him alive so that, in their words, he could "see what we are capable of." He later witnessed the entire village being herded into a church and burned alive. "I will never forget my grandfather's eyes," Art Tonoyan told the reporter. "He was a very sad person. I rarely remember him smiling. He never got over seeing his family murdered."[1]

As Tonoyan's family story shows, genocide, while directed at the destruction of larger groups, is a crime that is inextricably tied to families. What we hear repeatedly in the stories of survivors of twentieth-century genocides is the terrible way in which genocidal violence is embedded in the most sacred aspects of their family lives. This embedding is not just a matter of individual memory or of the transgenerational trauma that genocide can cause. It begins with genocide itself, with the intimate ways in which *génocidaires* target their victims. This is so much so that the perpetrators often become woven into the origin stories of survivors' families. We are acquainted with the two Turkish killers of Tonoyan's family, for example, because they addressed their young victim personally; they chose him to be the audience to their performance of genocidal violence, raping his mother and his sister in front of him before killing them. Embedded in this dramatization of their concept of power was a message—a message they were sending to him, as an Armenian child in 1915 Anatolia, and to the rest of the world; a message we are still receiving up to this day.

Unfortunately, the message witnessed by Tonoyan's grandfather is one that countless numbers of people have been forced to witness in the twentieth century alone. The scenario of power that the perpetrators enacted in front of the terrified little boy and their decision to let him live as a witness to their spectacle are characteristic of genocidal violence across widely disparate times and cultures. In this article I wish to examine this and other genocidal scenarios and the messages they are meant to send by looking at the integral role played by family institutions in genocidal patterns of violence. I argue that the crimes committed against Art Tonoyan's family members are examples of a specific kind of crime that can be called *life force atrocity*. For the purpose of definition, life force atrocity is a ritualized pattern of violence that targets the life force of a group by destroying both the physical symbols of its life force as well as its most basic institutions of reproduction, especially the family unit. It exists alongside and in conjunction with other, more frequently discussed, genocidal patterns of violence, and with them can act as evidence of an emerging genocidal logic during times of conflict.

The violent acts I will examine are often the most difficult to discuss, much less fathom. They involve two interrelated types of rituals: first, violent inversion rituals that seek to reverse proper hierarchies and relationships within families and thereby irrevocably to break sacred bonds. Such acts include forcing family members to watch the rape, torture, and murder of their loved ones and forcing them to participate in the perpetration of such crimes. The second type of ritual involved in genocidal violence against families is the ritual mutilation and desecration of symbols of group reproduction, including male and female reproductive organs, women's breasts as the sites of lactation, pregnant women as the loci of generative powers, and infants and small children as the sacred symbols of the group's future.[2]

This article will make the argument that understanding life force atrocities is crucial to understanding the genocidal process and how it differs from other instances of mass murder, most notably war. It treats life force atrocities outside of the frameworks of atrocity and rape in which they have long languished. Life force atrocities are not generic in nature, and they are not synonymous with "rape" or with "sexual violence," although they may involve both. They are directed at men as well as women, boys as well as girls, using each to inflict maximum damage to the spiritual core of those generative and foundational units we call families. They betray a specific state of mind among perpetrators, who are not merely engaged in killing but also in a subjective metaphysical struggle with the life force itself. When viewed from the perspective of life force atrocities, genocide appears to be a crime whose perpetrators are uniquely preoccupied with wresting power from that mysterious force that accounts for human life on this planet, a violent appropriation that they demonstrate in the highly symbolic ways in which they kill.

The Ritual Performance of Genocide

The types of atrocities that I am calling life force atrocities are often cited as incontrovertible evidence of perpetrator perversity—and they are certainly that. But our understanding of them should not be left at this, or we risk treating patterned violence as incidental and, in the process, making invisible a key feature of genocide. Instead, when we single out these acts for sustained analysis, we are able to offer another means of identifying genocidal intent in the absence of documentary proof. Just as the US Atrocities Documentation Team recently has identified village razing, cattle slaughtering, mass rape, and the use of racist epithets during killing in Darfur as de facto evidence of genocidal intent on the part of Janjaweed militias and the Government of Sudan,[3] the presence of specific acts of violence directed at families can also serve to alert us to the dangerous presence of genocidal logic in conflict situations—potentially at a very early stage in a conflict, before a full-blown root and branch genocide is in the works. Life force atrocities may signal—and act as evidence of—intent on the part of the state authorities in control of the conflict region, or they may offer a warning that a certain militia or cadre within an armed force is behaving genocidally.

[…]

As Christopher Browning has shown, the repeated performance of transgression—a performance that often includes mind-altering substances—can facilitate surprisingly quickly the normalization of atrocity by constructing new social realities and new values to go along with them.[4] In this way, genocidal rituals are formally very similar to non-genocidal and even normatively legitimate desensitization processes involved in training people to kill, whether they be ordinary soldiers or professional assassins. What distinguishes genocidal violence from other types of collective killing and brutality is the obsession it shows for the life force in all of its worldly manifestations. If we look at the details of the atrocities committed by the Hutu Interahamwe against young children, for example, the focused assault on several different aspects of the life force become clear: children as physical proof of the community's future, parental love and protectiveness as the bond that promotes family and communal unity, and sexual organs as the biological conduits of life-giving powers. This hostility towards symbolic and physical manifestations of the life force is a theme running through many if not most of the forms of torture used by *génocidaires* in the process of killing.

If genocidal rituals institutionalize the transgression of mundane social norms, they do so for the specific purpose of the destruction of a "national, ethnical, racial or religious group," to use the language of Article II of the UN Convention on the Crime of Genocide. The fact that perpetrators see their victims as part of a larger organic community explains why so much of the violence committed during genocides is deeply preoccupied with generative symbols. For perpetrators, these symbols—whether they are people of a specific status (such as mothers, "battle-age men," or religious figures) or relationships (such as marital, parental, or filial bonds)—are points of access to the ultimate threat, which is that power that continues to give birth to the community in the first place.

[…]

The Family Theater of Genocidal Violence

The fact is that much genocidal violence is committed *through* the small-scale institution of the family. *Génocidaires* often find their targets in family situations and take advantage of this to inflict the most severe tortures imaginable, essentially using the individual family as a symbolic stand-in for the group to be destroyed. But, despite the family-based location of much life force atrocity, the identification of genocides still tends to focus solely on the large-scale violence directed at the group.[5] This makes early identification of a potential genocide almost impossible and the final determination of genocide contingent upon large numbers or percentages of dead. One consequence of this is that cases in which a genocide was halted—such as in the case of the NATO intervention in Kosovo—there is little means of establishing empirically the presence of a specifically genocidal logic without access to clear statements of genocidal intent from the highest state and military authorities.

Focusing on families as the immediate representatives of the victim group can help us identify genocidal elements early on in conflicts, within smaller-scale massacres, before they reach the enormous proportions usually necessary to claim genocide.

[…]

Life Force Atrocities Without Genocide?

By way of conclusion, I would like to note that the particular forms of violence that I single out here as inherently genocidal are not necessarily confined to commonly recognized, root and branch, genocides. Inversion rituals and the ritual mutilation and desecration of sacred symbols of generation have been key features of recent wars in the Democratic Republic of Congo and Sierra Leone, to cite two examples from Africa.[6] They also played a significant role in Japan's occupation of East Asia in World War II and were particularly evident in Japan's Imperial Army's sex slavery system.[7] What does this mean about such violence being in and of itself evidence of genocidal intent?

One way to look at this question is to place life force atrocities within the longer-term reproductive process. Life force atrocities aim to compress total annihilation, which occurs over time, into one moment of ultimate destruction in which a group is destroyed in its past, present, and future tenses through targeting its temporal symbols—pregnant women, infants, the elderly—and undermining the bonds necessary for group cohesion and therefore for biological and cultural reproduction. Because life force atrocities are committed in immediate and clearly circumscribed social and political spaces—in a household, a front yard, a village square, a military encampment, and so forth—they become, for the perpetrators, microcosms of the potentially massive crime itself. The perpetrators of these crimes may or may not be acting according from directives received from higher authorities. Genocidal intent need not be institutionalized in a state or military in order for it to exit. Generally speaking, however, such institutionalization is necessary for the crime to reach the mass proportions that we associate with it.

[…]

Because genocide is rarely self-limiting, it is imperative that we learn to recognize genocidal patterns outside of state-sponsored genocides before we are presented with large numbers of dead. Life force atrocities offer one way of identifying evidence of possible genocide in the absence of clear statements on the parts of belligerents, and it can help analysts overcome accusations that the use of the term "genocide" is nothing more than a (highly politicized) matter of semantics. Precisely because of its destructive engagement with life forces, genocide tends to spread out from an initial target group and become an end in itself, a lifestyle, even, eventually causing massive suffering and regional instability. Because life force atrocities are the cause of such indescribable suffering and life-long trauma to survivors and their descendants, they demand swift intervention once they have been shown to constitute a pattern of warfare and communal violence.

Notes

1. Terri Jo Ryan, "Family Tree Tied to Forgotten Genocide," *Waco Tribune-Herald*, Sunday, 24 April 2005, http://www.aarweb.org/programs/awards/journalism_awards/winners/2006ryan.pdf (accessed 25 January 2010).

2. My use of the term "desecration" is drawn from Michael Sells' discussion of the treatment of Bosniak women by Serbian forces, something he also terms "gynocide." See Michael Sells, *The Bridge Betrayed: Religion and Genocide in Bosnia* (Berkeley: University of California Press, 1996).

3. See, for example, Stephen A. Kostas, "Making a Determination of Genocide in Darfur," in *Genocide in Darfur: Investigating the Atrocities in the Sudan*, ed. Samuel Totten and Eric Markusen, 111–26 (New York: Routledge, 2006).

4. Christopher R. Browning, *Ordinary Men: Reserve Battalion 101 and the Final Solution in Poland* (New York: HarperPerennial, 1998), esp. chapter 14, "The Jew Hunt" (121–32).

5. Stuart Stein, "Geno and Other Cides: A Cautionary Note on Knowledge Accumulation," in *Gendercide and Genocide*, ed. Adam Jones, 198–208 (Nashville, TN: Vanderbilt University Press, 2004).

6. *The Final Report of the Truth and Reconciliation Commission of Sierra Leone* (2007), http://www.sierra-leone.org/TRCDocuments.html (accessed 25 January 2010); Human Rights Watch, *Seeking Justice: The Prosecution of Sexual Violence in the Congo War* (2005), http://hrw.org/reports/2005/drc0305/index.htm (accessed 25 January 2010).

7. See, e.g., Iris Chang, *The Rape of Nanking: The Forgotten Holocaust of WWII* (New York: Basic Books, 1997); Sangmie Choi Schellstede, ed., *Comfort Women Speak: Testimony by Sex Slaves of the Japanese Military* (New York: Holmes & Meier, 2000); Yoshiaki Yoshimi, *Comfort Women* (New York: Columbia University Press, 2002).

9

War Produces Conditions for Genocide

Martin Shaw

Martin Shaw is a professor emeritus of international relations and politics at the University of Sussex in Brighton, England, who now serves as a research professor of international relations at the Institut Barcelona d'Estudis Internacionals and a professorial fellow in international relations and human rights at Roehampton University. He is the author of War and Genocide *(2003) and* What Is Genocide? *(2015).*

Because genocide is a type of social interaction and social relationship, a sociological framework is necessary and useful to explain genocide's connections with other social actions and structures. Martin Shaw recommends a framework that connects war with genocide. He argues that the term "genocide" was conceived in the context of war by Raphael Lemkin. Further, he argues that the war experience underpins the ideology that enables one to commit genocide. He cites examples connecting World War II and the Holocaust as well as World War I and the Armenian genocide, among others.

The study of genocide has generally been framed by legal and historical, rather than sociological perspectives. Law provided the impetus to the definition of the crime, through the pioneering efforts of Raphael Lemkin and the drafters of the United Nations Convention; it has continued to provide much of the drive towards

"War and Genocide: A Sociological Approach," by Martin Shaw, SciencesPo, November 4, 2007. Reprinted by permission.

recognition of recent genocides, in the work of the international criminal tribunals for former Yugoslavia and Rwanda. Historical studies account for the vast majority of genocide research, and have provided the main foundations for our knowledge. Yet law often provides too narrow a focus, separating genocide from the "crimes against humanity" and "war crimes" with which it is intimately linked, and concerned with individual criminal responsibility rather than explanation. And historical studies tend to highlight the particularity of certain events rather than the commonalities that lead us to define a range of actions, by collective actors in situations separated by time and space, as "genocide." Indeed, the majority of historical studies deal with a particular episode, the Holocaust, whose commonality with other genocides is often questioned by historians.

Genocide studies, therefore, require a sociological framework specifying that genocide is *a type of social action and social relationship* and explains its *typical connections with other types of social action and structure.* In recent books (Shaw 2003 and 2006), I have outlined a framework for understanding these two central and inter-related questions. My approach links genocide closely to war and it is this connection that is the primary focus of this article.

The Loss of the Connection Between War and Genocide

It is evident that genocide was first recognized in the context of war: the word was invented by Lemkin to describe atrocities against civilians under *Axis Rule in Occupied Europe* (the title of his foundational 1944 book). As he described it, genocide was "a concentrated and coordinated attack upon all the elements of nationhood" among the various occupied peoples. Genocide was a warlike campaign, occurring in the context of war, but fundamentally opposed to legitimate warfare:

> *"Genocide is the antithesis of the ... doctrine (…) [which] holds that war is directed against sovereigns and armies, not against*

subjects and civilians. In its modern application in civilized society, the doctrine means that war is conducted against states and armed forces and not against populations. It required a long period of evolution in civilized society to mark the way from wars of extermination, which occurred in ancient times and in the Middle Ages, to the conception of wars as being essentially limited to activities against armies and states." (Lemkin, 1944:80)

This seminal statement pinpointed the fact that identifying genocide as a criminal activity distinct from war still depended on the modern distinction between "civilized" and "uncivilized" warfare. Only by distinguishing between "sovereigns and armies" on the one hand, and "subjects and civilians" on the other, could genocide be differentiated from war. Although genocide should be defined as a crime *sui generis,* which might occur at least exceptionally in "peacetime" outside the context of more conventional warfare, it was in effect a new, modern form of the historic "wars of extermination."

These connections of genocide with war, in terms of context and meaning, remained central to the first legal uses of the idea. Only because genocide occurred in the context of an aggressive war did the United Nations consider themselves entitled to prosecute Nazi leaders for it at Nuremberg. Yet in the subsequent definition of genocide as the supreme international crime, the UN separated it from war. Thus, Resolution 96(I) of the General Assembly, adopted unanimously on 11 December 1946, defined genocide as "a denial of the right of existence of entire human groups, as homicide is the denial of the right to live of individual human beings." As William Schabas commented, this formulation eliminated "any nexus between genocide and armed conflict"; for him this was "the unfortunate legacy of the Nuremberg jurisprudence." However, there is reason to question whether this was such a fortunate move. Although it was certainly important to emphasize the fundamental difference of genocide from legitimate war, and the difference between a deliberate attack on a civilian population as such and crimes (against civilians or soldiers) committed in the course of otherwise legitimate war, these formulations, culminating in the 1948 Genocide Convention, also mitigated understanding of the deep connections between these different types of action.

Connections of Context and Causality

These connections can be defined as ones of *context*, and therefore *causality*; but also, more deeply, of *meaning*. The contextualization of genocide by war is manifest in most historical studies. Beginning with Nazism, it is evident how fundamentally this genocidal movement was defined by the experience of war and militaristic ideology. From its earliest street-fighting days the Nazi party defined political and social groups—Communists, Jews, homosexuals—as enemies linked in gigantic geopolitical conspiracies, to be "destroyed" in a quasi-military sense. And although genocidal policies began as the Nazi regime consolidated its control over German society, it was only as it moved into aggressive war that the most generally murderous phases began. Only with the launching of war did the regime feel able to coolly terminate the lives of disabled Germans, freeing up hospital capacity for others deemed more essential to the fight. Only then, too, did Nazism gain a hold over large numbers of Poles, whom it regarded as inferior, and with them the largest Jewish populations in Europe. Under the cover of aggression and large military movements it was possible to destroy historic communities, herding Poles eastwards and Jews into ghettos. And only as total war became ever more extreme, in the invasion of the Soviet Union, did Nazi policy move towards physical extermination of enemies such as Communists, Gypsies and above all Jews.

Similar contexts apply in other major genocidal episodes. The Young Turk regime in the Ottoman Empire targeted the Armenians during the First World War, seeing them both as potential allies of the Russian enemy and as obstacles to the kind of Turkish nation they wanted to create. The Soviet regime destroyed the Chechen and Volga German peoples during the Second World War, seeing them as potential allies of the Nazi enemy. The Khmer Rouge concluded their war against the US-backed Lon Nol regime by instituting the first phase of genocide against urban and educated sections of the population, together with ethnic and national minorities. More recently, Serbian nationalists launched their wars in the former Yugoslavia by destroying Croat and Bosnian Muslim communities. Rwandan Hutu nationalists launched their genocide of the opposition and the Tutsi population while their regime was facing successful armed incursions by the Rwandan Patriotic Front. Serbia launched its destruction of the Kosovo Albanian community in response to Kosovo Liberation Army attacks, and especially NATO's bombing.

These examples and others support the idea of close links between genocide and war. Certainly, genocidal episodes do occur outside the context of conventional war, although even these tend to be directed by militaristic regimes, such as the campaigns of Stalin's Russia and Mao's China against peasants and national minorities. These regimes had recent histories of civil war and viewed social groups in the fashion of armed enemies. However, these examples caution against any simple idea of "war" itself as a cause of genocide; indeed the many cases of genocide in wartime do not tell us why some wars see genocides and some parties in wars commit genocide, and others do not. All that these many cases do is to point overwhelmingly to the centrality of these linkages, underlining the misconception involved in trying to separate genocide from war, conceptually or causally, in any definitive way.

Connections of Meaning

If it is not "war" itself that is causal, nevertheless, *ideas* of war are important in the production of genocide. It occurs when an organized, armed collective actor comes to define a social group or population as an *enemy*, not merely in a political but in an essentially military sense, i.e. as an enemy *to be destroyed*. Hence the continuing relevance of Lemkin's early formulation of genocide as illegitimate war, and the significance of the common element of *destruction* in the definitions of war and of genocide. War, following Clausewitz, is the destruction by one armed actor of an armed enemy, its power and its will to resist. Genocide is the destruction by an armed actor of an *unarmed* social group, its power and its will to resist. Hence the significance for understanding genocide of the distinctions (drawn from the law, philosophy and theory of war) between armed and unarmed (civilians), between organized military power and (militarily unorganized) social and cultural power, and between conventional military resistance and civilian resistance.

Genocide as action means something very similar to war, except that it is directed by one type of actor at another very different type—whereas in "normal" war the opposed actors are of the same organized military type, however else they may differ. But just as war is not merely something that one actor does to another, so genocide involves *relationships* between the armed and unarmed actors. Genocide is often thought of as something "perpetrators" do to "victims," but in reality it is also a form of social *conflict*, however unequal and distorted, so that perpetrators must take account of victims' responses, and *vice versa*. The idea of genocide without resistance of any kind, if only in the minds of "helpless" victims or through proxies, is absurd, a *reductio ad absurdam* of the "one-sided" character of genocide.

Changing Structures of Warfare and Contemporary Genocide

If we can map—with crucial differences—the ideas of war on to the forms of genocidal action and conflict, then clearly we must explore the ways in which specific forms of warfare, in different periods, are instrumental in creating possibilities of genocide. Moving from the meaning of genocide to its *causality*, the *structures* of war will be central. Except in the case of the most highly militarized regimes, and indeed often even in those cases, the operational destruction of a social group rarely takes place, or at least does not reach its most extreme phases, until the perpetrator state or movement is engaged in extensive armed conflict. Where armed forces, whether conventional or party/movement-based, are already mobilized and using violence, it is easier to re-direct them against civilians. Indeed, where armed men are already using violence against civilians in the pursuit of more or less conventional war against other armed forces, it is easier to mobilize them against particular civilian groups as such.

Historically this has suggested, of course, that modern *total warfare*, developed in the late nineteenth and twentieth centuries through extensive physical, economic, social, cultural and ideological mobilization of populations, particularly facilitated genocide. Although, as Lemkin noted, the idea of a "war of extermination" has longer historical antecedents, modern genocide is the product of modern war. Although not all sides in all wars have practiced genocide, of course, the *common* structure of total warfare, in which mobilizing whole populations leads to these populations becoming targets, makes it easier for genocidal States and movements, in their ideologies, to designate specific groups of civilian populations as enemies in themselves.

Recognizing this important structural feature of twentieth-century warfare naturally leads to asking whether and how, as warfare has changed, patterns of genocide have also been modified. The decline of total-war mobilization in advanced industrial states, and indeed of war itself between major states in the international system, as well as the disappearance of classically totalitarian states, all appear to be associated with a decline in large-scale, ideologically intensive and multi-targeted genocidal episodes. On the other hand, the fragmentation of old empires into larger numbers of nation-states has been associated with an extension of the long-standing trend towards ethnic homogenization, so that genocidal expulsion (often recognized under the euphemistic label 'ethnic cleansing') may actually have become more widespread. The emergence of *global surveillance warfare* means that local States and armed movements have to engage with extensive international political, legal and media monitoring of their activities, but so far this has stimulated new practices of manipulation and denial by genocidal political forces, rather than any general inhibition of genocide. For example, the normalization of electoral democracy in the global order has generated an incentive to murderous expulsion, as regimes have sought to homogenize their electorates. Likewise, the global media impact of spectacular terrorist atrocities against unarmed populations has encouraged relatively weak armed networks to make civilians their prime targets, thus pushing contemporary forms of guerrilla warfare in ever-more genocidal directions.

10

Hannah Arendt Was Wrong: Nazi Evil Was Not Banal

Thomas White

Thomas White is a Wiley Journal contributing author. His philosophical and theological writings have appeared both in print and online.

The German-Jewish philosopher Hannah Arendt attended the war crimes trial of Adolph Eichmann in Israel in 1961 as a reporter for the New Yorker. *Her resulting articles painted Eichmann as a rather ordinary person who organized the transportation of millions of Jews and others to their deaths. She referred to this as "the banality of evil." Thomas White argues, with textual evidence from leading scholars, that Arendt's use of "the banality of evil" was not only controversial but also flawed.*

Can one *do* evil without *being* evil? This was the puzzling question that the philosopher Hannah Arendt grappled with when she reported for *The New Yorker* in 1961 on the war crimes trial of Adolph Eichmann, the Nazi operative responsible for organising the transportation of millions of Jews and others to various concentration camps in support of the Nazi's Final Solution.

Arendt found Eichmann an ordinary, rather bland, bureaucrat, who in her words, was "neither perverted nor sadistic," but

"What Did Hannah Arendt Really Mean by the Banality of Evil?" by Thomas White, Aeon Media Group Ltd., April 23, 2018, https://aeon.co/ideas/what-did-hannah-arendt-really-mean-by-the-banality-of-evil. Licensed under CC BY-ND 4.0.

"terrifyingly normal." He acted without any motive other than to diligently advance his career in the Nazi bureaucracy. Eichmann was not an amoral monster, she concluded in her study of the case, *Eichmann in Jerusalem: A Report on the Banality of Evil* (1963). Instead, he performed evil deeds without evil intentions, a fact connected to his "thoughtlessness," a disengagement from the reality of his evil acts. Eichmann "never realised what he was doing" due to an "inability… to think from the standpoint of somebody else." Lacking this particular cognitive ability, he "commit[ted] crimes under circumstances that made it well-nigh impossible for him to know or to feel that he [was] doing wrong."

Arendt dubbed these collective characteristics of Eichmann "the banality of evil": he was not inherently evil, but merely shallow and clueless, a "joiner," in the words of one contemporary interpreter of Arendt's thesis: he was a man who drifted into the Nazi Party, in search of purpose and direction, not out of deep ideological belief. In Arendt's telling, Eichmann reminds us of the protagonist in Albert Camus's novel *The Stranger* (1942), who randomly and casually kills a man, but then afterwards feels no remorse. There was no particular intention or obvious evil motive: the deed just "happened."

This wasn't Arendt's first, somewhat superficial impression of Eichmann. Even 10 years after his trial in Israel, she wrote in 1971:

> *I was struck by the manifest shallowness in the doer [ie Eichmann] which made it impossible to trace the uncontestable evil of his deeds to any deeper level of roots or motives. The deeds were monstrous, but the doer—at least the very effective one now on trial—was quite ordinary, commonplace, and neither demonic nor monstrous.*

The banality-of-evil thesis was a flashpoint for controversy. To Arendt's critics, it seemed absolutely inexplicable that Eichmann could have played a key role in the Nazi genocide yet have no evil intentions. Gershom Scholem, a fellow philosopher (and theologian), wrote to Arendt in 1963 that her banality-of-evil thesis was merely a slogan that "does not impress me, certainly, as the product of profound analysis." Mary McCarthy, a novelist and good friend of Arendt, voiced sheer incomprehension: "[I]t seems to me that what you are saying is that Eichmann lacks an inherent human quality: the capacity for thought, consciousness—conscience. But then isn't he a monster simply?"

The controversy continues to the present day. The philosopher Alan Wolfe, in *Political Evil: What It Is and How to Combat It* (2011), criticised Arendt for "psychologising"—that is, avoiding—the issue of evil as evil by defining it in the limited context of Eichmann's humdrum existence. Wolfe argued that Arendt concentrated too much on *who* Eichmann was, rather than *what* Eichmann did. For Arendt's critics, this focus on Eichmann's insignificant, banal life seemed to be an 'absurd digression' from his evil deeds.

Other recent critics have documented Arendt's historical errors, which led her to miss a deeper evil in Eichmann, when she claimed that his evil was "thought-defying," as Arendt wrote to the philosopher Karl Jaspers three years after the trial. The historian Deborah Lipstadt, the defendant in David Irving's Holocaust-denial libel trial, decided in 2000, cites documentation released by the Israeli government for use in the legal proceeding. It proves, Lipstadt asserts in *The Eichmann Trial* (2011), that Arendt's use of the term "banal" was flawed:

> *The memoir [by Eichmann] released by Israel for use in my trial reveals the degree to which Arendt was wrong about Eichmann. It is permeated with expressions of Nazi ideology... [Eichmann] accepted and espoused the idea of racial purity.*

Lipstadt further argues that Arendt failed to explain why Eichmann and his associates would have attempted to destroy evidence of their war crimes, if he was indeed unaware of his wrongdoing.

In *Eichmann Before Jerusalem* (2014), the German historian Bettina Stangneth reveals another side to him besides the banal, seemingly apolitical man, who was just acting like any other "ordinary" career-oriented bureaucrat. Drawing on audiotapes of interviews with Eichmann by the Nazi journalist William Sassen,

Stangneth shows Eichmann as a self-avowed, aggressive Nazi ideologue strongly committed to Nazi beliefs, who showed no remorse or guilt for his role in the Final Solution—a radically evil Third Reich operative living inside the deceptively normal shell of a bland bureaucrat. Far from being "thoughtless," Eichmann had plenty of thoughts—thoughts of genocide, carried out on behalf of his beloved Nazi Party. On the tapes, Eichmann admitted to a sort of Jekyll-and-Hyde dualism:

> I, "[t]he cautious bureaucrat," that was me, yes indeed. But … this cautious bureaucrat was attended by a … a fanatical [Nazi] warrior, fighting for the freedom of my blood, which is my birthright…

Arendt completely missed this radically evil side of Eichmann when she wrote 10 years after the trial that there was "no sign in him of firm ideological convictions or of specific evil motives." This only underscores the banality—and falsity—of the banality-of-evil thesis. And though Arendt never said that Eichmann was just an innocent "cog" in the Nazi bureaucracy, nor defended Eichmann as "just following orders"—both common misunderstandings of her findings on Eichmann—her critics, including Wolfe and Lipstadt, remain unsatisfied.

So what should we conclude about Arendt's claim that Eichmann (as well as other Germans) *did* evil without *being* evil?

The question is a puzzle because Arendt missed an opportunity to investigate the larger meaning of Eichmann's particular evil by not expanding her study of him into a broader study of evil's nature. In *The Origins of Totalitarianism* (1951), published well before the Eichmann trial, Arendt said:

> It is inherent in our entire [Western] philosophical tradition that we cannot conceive of a 'radical evil'…

Instead of using the Eichmann case as a way forward to advance the tradition's understanding of radical evil, Arendt decided that his evil was banal, that is, "thought-defying." By taking a narrow legalistic, formalistic approach to the trial—she emphasised that there were no deeper issues at stake beyond the legal facts of Eichmann's guilt or innocence—Arendt automatically set herself up for failure as to the deeper why of Eichmann's evil.

Yet in her writings before *Eichmann in Jerusalem*, she actually took an opposite position. In *The Origins of Totalitarianism*, she argued that the evil of the Nazis was absolute and inhuman, *not* shallow and incomprehensible, the metaphorical embodiment of hell itself: "[T]he reality of concentration camps resembles nothing so much as medieval pictures of Hell."

By declaring in her pre-Eichmann trial writings that absolute evil, exemplified by the Nazis, was driven by an audacious, monstrous intention to abolish humanity itself, Arendt was echoing the spirit of philosophers such as F W J Schelling and Plato, who did not shy away from investigating the deeper, more demonic aspects of evil. But this view changed when Arendt met Eichmann, whose bureaucratic emptiness suggested no such diabolical profundity, but only prosaic careerism and the "inability to think." At that point, her earlier imaginative thinking about moral evil was distracted, and the "banality of evil" slogan was born. Moreover, Arendt died in 1975: perhaps if she had lived longer she could have clarified the puzzles surrounding the banality-of-evil thesis, which still confound critics to this day. But this we shall never know.

Thus we are left with her original thesis as it stands. What is the basic confusion behind it? Arendt never did reconcile her impressions of Eichmann's bureaucratic banality with her earlier searing awareness of the evil, inhuman acts of the Third Reich. She saw the ordinary-looking functionary, but not the ideologically evil warrior. How Eichmann's humdrum life could co-exist with that "other" monstrous evil puzzled her. Nevertheless, Arendt never downplayed Eichmann's guilt, repeatedly described him as a war criminal, and concurred with his death sentence as handed down by the Israeli court. Though Eichmann's motives were, for her, obscure and thought-defying, his genocidal acts were not. In the final analysis, Arendt *did* see the true horror of Eichmann's evil.

11

Recognition of the Armenian Genocide Could Strengthen Turkey's Position

David Tolbert

David Tolbert has served as president of the International Center for Transitional Justice since 2010. Prior to this appointment, he held positions that include assistant secretary-general and special expert to the UN Secretary-General on United Nations Assistance to the Khmer Rouge trials, as well as deputy chief prosecutor of the International Criminal Tribunal for the former Yugoslavia.

Turkey has yet to acknowledge its role in the genocide of its Armenian population between 1915 and 1917. Turkey holds the highest number of judgments against it for violation of human rights, and David Tolbert argues that this denial and lack of public apology continue to denigrate the Armenians and work against the country's best interests. For example, recognition could strengthen and make legitimate Turkey's position on the world stage. To take such steps would also demonstrate a commitment to the protection of human rights.

On April 24, we commemorate the 100th anniversary of the Armenian genocide. On that date in 1915, some 250 Armenian political leaders and intellectuals were arrested and subsequently tortured and murdered by Ottoman Turkish authorities, effectively launching the genocide in which approximately 1.5 million

"The Armenian Genocide: 100 Years of Denial (And Why It's in Turkey's Interest to End It)," by David Tolbert, International Center for Transitional Justice, April 24, 2015. Reprinted by permission.

Armenians were systematically murdered. This grim centenary marks not only the crime itself but also a century of its denial by the Turkish state and wide swaths of Turkish society.

Denial is the final fortress of those who commit genocide and other mass crimes. Perpetrators hide the truth in order to avoid accountability and protect the political and economic advantages they sought to gain by mass killings and theft of the victims' property, and to cement the new reality by manufacturing an alternative history. Recent studies have established that such denial not only damages the victims and their destroyed communities, it promises a future based on lies, sowing the seeds of future conflict, repression and suffering.

The facts of the Armenian genocide are well known and documented, and any honest debate is not about whether the genocide happened but about the exact number of murdered, the worth of their stolen property and the long-term impact of this crime.

The Ottoman authorities of the day (the government of the Committee of Union and Progress (CUP), often referred to as the Young Turks) and their allies carried out the systematic murder of some 1.5 million Armenians between 1915 and 1917, destroying a large percentage of the Armenian population in the Ottoman Empire at that time. Then, from 1918 to 1923, many of the surviving Armenians and others, including Greeks and Assyrians, were driven from their homes, robbed of their remaining possessions, starved, and murdered.[1] Like other genocides, the mass killing of Armenians was hardly spontaneous. It was planned and executed with efficiency, without mercy.

Turkey's Culture of Denial and Its Spoils

A hundred years on, despite a mountain of evidence, there remains a culture of official denial in Turkey. In a pallid public statement "on the events of 1915," President Recep Tayyip Erdoğan recently extended "[Turkey's] condolences to [the] grandchildren" of the Armenians "who lost their lives in the context of the early twentieth century." Rubbing salt in the wounds, he trivialized the suffering caused to Armenians at the time by equating them to that of "every other citizen of the Ottoman Empire."[2] Considering the scale of the slaughter and the nature of the genocidal effort directed at Armenians, Erdogan's attempts to equate their suffering to that of "every citizen of the Ottoman Empire" constitutes a form of denial in itself.

Although such rhetoric is not new, the culture of denial in some respects has intensified in Turkey over the years. In 1919, albeit under international pressure, the Ottoman authorities established a tribunal that convicted two senior district officials for deporting Armenians and acting "against humanity and civilization." The tribunal found that the perpetrators and their co-conspirators had executed a top-down, carefully crafted plan, specifically finding:

> *The disaster visiting the Armenians was not a local or isolated event. It was the result of a premeditated decision taken by a central body; [...] and the immolations and excesses which took place were based on oral and written orders issued by that central body.*[3]

However, a few years later, after a new government was formed in Ankara, the Nationalists annulled all of the sentences.[4] Moreover, in another crime against humanity, pursuant to the orders of Kemal Ataturk, who later became the President of the Republic of Turkey, Armenians who remained in the western Cilicia region of Turkey were expelled, along with the Greek and Assyrian populations. Several high-level perpetrators of the genocide became senior leaders in Turkey and others were celebrated as national heroes.[5]

While it is argued that the culture of denial arose as a result of the close connection that the Armenian genocide has with the birth of modern Turkey,[6] this is an explanation of possible causes, not a justification for the most serious of crimes. A parallel can be drawn with the conquest of the Americas by the United States and the continental powers in their multitudinous abuses and genocidal killings of Native Americans: the explanation may be the rapacious hunger for land, but it is not a defense for the crimes committed. Looking for such justification for these systematic crimes amounts to a strategy of normalization and denial.

A closer look at Turkey's refusal to reckon with the truth about the genocide invites two important questions: How is denial perpetuated? And how does a society move beyond denial?

Before these questions can be addressed, some understanding of how denial is formulated and promulgated is required. Israel Charny has pointed to a "template of denial," which owes much to the Turkish handling of the Armenian genocide. He identifies a number of rules (or in more contemporary terms a kind of playbook), on how to get away with genocide, including: Do not acknowledge that the genocide took place; transform it into other kinds of events; portray the victims as the perpetrators; insist more victims were from the perpetrator's group; and relativize the genocide in whatever way possible.[7]

A key element of any effort to deny genocide is to try to reinterpret international laws and conventions, to say that the crimes do not fit the legal definition of genocide,[8] thus rendering the crime not so serious after all. As if the mass killing of 1.5 million human beings does not scream out for justice, regardless of the state of the law at the time.

This twisting of legal language is hardly limited to Turkey. It has many imitators, from the Nazis to the Khmer Rouge.

Another of Turkey's tactics is to pressure other states not to recognize the genocide. In the latest development, Turkey recalled its ambassador to the Vatican for "consultations" just hours after Pope Francis referred to the mass killing of Armenians as the "first genocide of the twentieth century." Turkey was successful in lobbying members of the US Congress during the Reagan and Bush administrations to defeat congressional resolutions that would have made April 24 a national day of remembrance.[9] However, it is noteworthy that such pressure failed in other cases, and dozens of countries, including Argentina, France, Greece and Russia, have all officially recognized the Armenian genocide, despite Turkey's threats and reprisals.

Another ploy in the denier's bag of tricks is to manipulate statistics, downplaying the number of victims (or, in this case, the number of Armenians who lived in the Ottoman Empire in 1915), and destroy official documents.

The genocide of the Armenians proved to be an opening act in a century replete with mass extermination: from the furnaces of Auschwitz to the killing fields of Cambodia to the genocide in Rwanda (marked earlier this month by its 21st anniversary) to the slaughterhouse of Bosnia and too much of the barbarity that we see in the world today. The butchers have learned the lessons all too well.

Hitler himself took succor in the genocide of the Armenians and famously remarked: "Who, after all, speaks today of the annihilation of the Armenians?" Hitler learned the lessons of the Armenian genocide well and drew on them as he planned the extermination of Jews and other groups that stood in the way of his murderous vision of "Aryan superiority."

Consequences of Denial and Benefits of Acknowledgement

The consequences of denial are deep and lasting, not only for the descendants of the Armenians, but also for Turkey itself, in large and small ways. Putting perpetrators of genocide in the Turkish pantheon of national heroes has its price.

While we must be careful not to draw too direct a line from the Armenian genocide to all of Turkey's current problems, we would be remiss not to take account of Turkey's poor current human rights record and its history of substandard treatment of minorities within its borders.[10]

Indeed, Turkey today bears the dubious distinction of having the highest number of judgments for violation of human rights rendered against it by the European Court of Human Rights.[11] It is criticized for legislating such vague and groundless crimes such as "insulting Turkish identity,"[12] which has now been reformed to "denigration of the Turkish nation, the state of the Republic of

Turkey, the Turkish Parliament (TBMM), the government of the Republic of Turkey and the legal institutions of the state."

Even Orhan Pamuk, the Turkish Nobel Laureate, faced an official order for his books to be removed from the shelves of public libraries and burned after he referenced the Armenian genocide to a Swiss newspaper. These are not actions of a state grounded in the rule of law and human rights.

There is a different path to follow, one traveled by other countries with as heavy or heavier burdens of history, and it points to approaches that might be useful for Turkey.

The first step includes ending the politics of denial and embracing acknowledgement. One need only think of the experience of post-war Germany, which, despite the Nuremberg trials, spent several decades (at best) ignoring, if not denying, the massive crimes of the Nazi period. Over time though, West Germany and then a reunited Germany began to deal with the horrendous crimes of the Holocaust through important trials, such as those held in Frankfurt in the 1960s, which exposed the awful crimes committed in Auschwitz in chilling detail.

The German government opened up archives to the public, provided reparations to victims (or their descendants) and constructed memorials to affect public remembrance and acknowledgement.

Over time, it began to remove some of the culprits from the police, military and political ranks, and importantly reformed its political legal institutions. In one of the most iconic acts of acknowledgement, Chancellor Willy Brandt went to his knees in front of a monument dedicated to victims of the Warsaw Ghetto. It was a symbolic act that spoke of contrition and apology; it carried enormous significance and meaning for the victims and their survivors as well as the world at large.

Germany is not alone, other countries have moved past the stage of denial, whether expressed or implied, to address the violations of the past. We are now celebrating the 30th anniversary of Nunca Mas ("Never Again"), the final report of an official effort to document the vast system of enforced disappearances perpetrated in Argentina during the military dictatorship and "Dirty War," which led to trials of some of the most responsible perpetrators and a much clearer understanding of that dark period in the country's history. We have seen similar experiences in much of Latin America, through truth commissions, other commissions of inquiry and historical clarification, trials, and reparation programs.

Some countries have taken other approaches to uncovering their sordid histories. In South Africa, the history and abuses of apartheid were partly exposed through the Truth and Reconciliation Commission. Many countries in eastern and central Europe have pursued processes of lustration (or vetting) after the Cold War, exposing and penalizing those behind state-sponsored abuses. In the former Yugoslavia, denial is still strong in some places regarding crimes like the genocide in Srebrenica; yet, trials at the national and international levels have established the culpability of many of the perpetrators and helped get the truth to the public.

There are many other experiences to draw on, and they all point to the importance of acknowledgment of both genocide and other serious crimes and the state's failure to protect its citizens. In the case of Turkey, where there are no perpetrators of the genocide presently alive, criminal trials have no role left to play; that makes it all the more important that criminal processes not be turned against those who tell the truth, who expose the genocide and speak for the victims, as in the case of Pamuk.

That would be a small but significant step toward addressing Turkey's historic debt to the Armenians and one expected of a country that proclaims to be a member of the family of modern democracies.

An important first step would be for President Erdoğan to apologize to the Armenian community for the genocide. A tepid statement using euphemisms like "the events of 1915" only makes matters worse. He is in a strong position in Turkey, and politically he can afford to take this morally right action. It is his duty as president of all citizens of the country to set the record straight.

Official contrition would help in healing the deep injuries and damage suffered by the Armenian community, in Armenia and in the diaspora. Such an apology ought to be accompanied by measures to establish full diplomatic relations with the Republic of Armenia, which would be a meaningful goodwill gesture.

The benefits of such an act would not only be directed at Armenians, but at Turkey itself. By acknowledging these crimes, the Turkish state would send a message to the many minorities within its borders and to all of its citizens that the state takes their rights and the rule of law seriously. It would also be a signal that when the state violates or fails to protect its citizens' rights, the Turkish authorities would provide a remedy to them, in line with international law.

More broadly, Turkey has an important role to play internationally and regionally and the recognition of the genocide would, in the long term, make the country appear stronger and more trustworthy to all.

Its current position is not only morally unsustainable but undermines its position as an honest partner and a legitimate regional power. A break with the current policy of denial would show the maturity of Turkish democracy and could help to increase regional stability. The potential impact of an apology on its neighbors, notably the Republic of Armenia, would open the possibility for dialogue and strengthen Turkey's role in the region regarding unresolved issues like Nagorno-Karabakh.

Not only would this apology send an important message inside Turkey and to its neighbors, it is a message that would resonate well beyond the borders of the country. In the Balkans, where Turkey has increasing sway, denial is alive and well, and presents a significant obstacle to re-establishing confidence between former warring parties, such as Serbia, Bosnia and Herzegovina, Croatia and Kosovo. An act of acknowledgement would substantially increase Turkey's ability to mediate and support initiatives in contexts where impunity reigns, from Israel and Palestine to Syria to Sudan and many other places.

If Turkey and President Erdoğan were serious about reversing the culture of denial, there is more to do. A crucial measure would be to establish a truthful and accurate historical record of what happened to the Armenians. This could be in the form of an official Commission of Historical Clarification, composed of impartial and respected experts, which would examine the historical record and issue a report that would accurately reflect the history of the period and establish how the crimes were committed. Such a commission would need to be composed of experts that were objective, credible and fair minded.

Using international commissioners or a mixture of international and national experts, which has occurred in a number of truth commissions and other processes, would add considerable credibility to the process. The Commission for the Truth in El Salvador and the Commission for Historical Clarification in Guatemala are good examples of mixed national-international commissions. Such a commission should build on the work of the earlier unofficial Turkish Armenian Reconciliation Commission.

Some form of reparations for the Armenian community in Turkey would have to be provided. After all, the plunder of their property enriched the modern Turkish state. While too much time may have passed for individual reparations to be awarded, projects could be undertaken to support Armenian communities inside and outside of Turkey to address their material needs and, at least symbolically, their losses. Symbolic reparations in the form of monuments and memorials can serve an important purpose in recognizing victims and helping to remind the affected communities that the state acknowledges its failures and will guard against these abuses happening again.

Perhaps most important, Turkey can demonstrate a serious commitment to reforming laws and institutions that are meant to protect the human rights of all of its citizens. In doing so, the state would find effective ways to improve its weak record on these issues in the courts in Strasbourg and beyond. It would also send a message to its citizens that the crimes like those perpetrated against Armenians would never be permitted in contemporary Turkey.

There is no doubt many other steps could and should be taken in the Turkish case, but the process would best begin with an apology and acknowledgement by President Erdoğan. He need not go on his knees like Willy Brandt, for he is his own person, but in his own way he needs to apologize on behalf of the Turkish state, to say "never again." In doing so he would personify a new Turkey, one determined to heed the warning sounded by Israel Charny: "We must fight denials because the denial of genocide is . . . a process which is intended to desensitize and make[s] possible the emergence of new forms of genocidal violence to peoples in the future."[13]

Notes

1 Sara Cohan, "A Brief History of the Armenian Genocide," *Social Education 69*, no. 6 (2005): 336–337.

2 Samantha Power, *A Problem from Hell: America and the Age of Genocide*, c2002., 14.

3 Ibid., 15.

4 Alayarian, *Consequences of Denial*, 17–18.

5 Kévorkian, *The Armenian Genocide*, 811.

6 Ibid., 807–812.

7 Roger W. Smith, Eric Markusen, and Robert Jay Lifton, "Professional Ethics and the Denial of Armenian Genocide," *Holocaust and Genocide Studies 9*, no. 1 (March 20, 1995): 11.

8 See, for instance, Michael M. Gunter, *Armenian History and the Question of Genocide* (Palgrave Macmillan, 2011), chap. 2. It is worth noting that in a very legal narrow sense, the term genocide has its limits: the massive killings in Cambodia—some 25%–40% of the population was exterminated, but because they were largely of same ethnic group, the killings fall into the category of crimes against humanity, rather than genocide.

9 Smith, Markusen, and Lifton, "Professional Ethics and the Denial of Armenian Genocide," 4.

10 See, for instance, the Human Rights Committee Concluding Observations on the initial report of Turkey adopted by the Committee at its 106th session (15 October–2 November 2012), UN Doc. CCPR/C/TUR/CO/1, 13 November 2010.

11 See Annual Report 2013 of the European Court of Human Rights, Council of Europe, 203. From 1959 to 2013, there are 2,639 judgments against Turkey in which at least one violation has been found by the Court.

12 Alayarian, *Consequences of Denial*, 129.

13 Israel W. Charny, "The psychological satisfaction of denials of the Holocaust or other genocides by non-extremists or bigots, and even by known scholars," IDEA J SOC 1 (2001).

12

Auschwitz Evidence Causes Judge to Rule Against David Irving, Holocaust Denier

Steve Busfield

Steve Busfield is a former news, sports, and business journalist for the Guardian. *His freelance work has also appeared on Yahoo, Forbes .com, and elsewhere.*

In 1994, Penguin Books published the American Holocaust scholar Deborah Lipstadt's book Denying the Holocaust: The Growing Assault on Truth and Memory. *Historian David Irving later claimed that this book created a wave of hatred against him by labeling him a Holocaust denier. He brought a libel suit against her in his native Britain. Steve Busfield reports on the outcome of the case, which Irving lost. Key to the judge's verdict was testimony about whether Jewish deaths were conducted on a massive or modest scale. He found no serious historian could doubt that hundreds of thousands of deaths occurred in the gas chambers of Auschwitz.*

H istorian David Irving has lost his emotive libel case against the American academic who accused him of denying the scale of the Holocaust.

After considering the case for almost four weeks, Judge Charles Gray ruled against Mr Irving, saying he had failed to prove his reputation had been damaged.

"Irving Loses Holocaust Libel Case," by Steve Busfield, Guardian News and Media Limited, April 11, 2000. Reprinted by permission.

Mr Irving, who outraged survivors of Nazi death camps, was seeking damages over Professor Deborah Lipstadt's 1994 book, *Denying the Holocaust: The Growing Assault on Truth and Memory*, which he claimed had generated waves of hatred against him.

Professor Lipstadt and her publishers, Penguin Books, both denied libelling Mr Irving by branding him "a Holocaust denier" in a book which attacked revisionists alleged to have denied or played down the slaughter of 6m Jews during the second world war.

Under British law, Prof Lipstadt and her co-defendant were not able to rely solely on truth as a defence.

Both sides had been told the verdict yesterday, leaving the announcement of the result in court today somewhat muted. The historian left through the rear entrance of the law courts, accompanied by high court security staff, saying only that the judge's ruling was "perverse."

Mr Irving, who is now likely to face defence costs estimated at £2m, Irving, indicated that he would appeal against the verdict, though he refused to talk about the effect of meeting the potentially crippling costs.

"Why is everyone talking about money, I'm not interested in money. It is all about reputation," he said. But when asked if he had sufficient funds to cover the bills he answered simply: "No."

A statement issued by Professor Lipstadt said: "I never had any doubts that [the ruling] would be [in our favour] but nonetheless, I am gratified.

"I hope that this victory will save other authors from having to face such trials and tribulations.

"I see this not only as a personal victory, but also as a victory for all those who speak out against hate and prejudice. It was a struggle for truth and for memory and a fight against those who sow the seeds of racism and anti-semitism. They have pursued justice not just on my, but on many people's behalf."

Eldred Tabachnik QC, president of the Board of Deputies of British Jews, welcomed the judgment.

He said: "The board is pleased that David Irving's action against Professor Lipstadt and her publisher Penguin Books has been so clearly rejected by the British courts. The decision proves that David Irving is a falsifier of history. Irving follows the short line of Holocaust deniers who aim to resurrect Nazism by denying the planned destruction of the European Jews.

"Although the Holocaust itself was not an issue at the trial, we welcome the fact that attempts to manipulate the truth about the tragic events of that time have been shown to be baseless."

Mr Justice Gray said the charges he had found to be substantially true were that "Irving had for his own ideological reasons persistently and deliberately misrepresented and manipulated historical evidence" and that "for the same reasons, he had portrayed Hitler in an unwarrantedly favourable light, principally in relation to his attitude towards and responsibility for the treatment of the Jews."

The judge said he found that Irving was "an active Holocaust denier; that he was anti-Semitic and racist and that he associated with right-wing extremists who promoted neo-Nazism."

There were certain defamatory imputations which he had found to be defamatory of Mr Irving, but in his judgment the charges against Mr Irving which had been proved to be true were of "sufficient gravity" for it to be clear that the failure to prove the truth of other matters did not have any material effect on the historian's reputation.

The judge observed that Mr Irving's submissions appeared to him "to have a distinct air of unreality about them." In the instances he had found the defendants' criticisms to be justified, Mr Irving had "treated the historical evidence in a manner which fell far short of the standard to be expected of a conscientious historian.

"Irving in those respects misrepresented and distorted the evidence which was available to him," he added.

On the issue of Auschwitz, the judge said the central question to be determined in the case was whether or not the evidence supported the defendants' contention that the number of deaths ran into hundreds of thousands or whether Mr Irving was right when he claimed that the killing by gas was on a modest scale.

He commented: "I have to confess that, in common I suspect with most other people, I had supposed that the evidence of mass extermination of Jews in the gas chambers at Auschwitz was compelling.

"I have, however, set aside this preconception when assessing the evidence adduced by the parties in these proceedings." He said it appeared to him that the cumulative effect of the documentary evidence for the genocidal operation of gas chambers at Auschwitz was "considerable."

He concluded: "Having considered the various arguments advanced by Irving to assail the effect of the convergent evidence relied on by the defendants, it is my conclusion that no objective, fair-minded historian would have serious cause to doubt that there were gas chambers at Auschwitz and that they were operated on a substantial scale to kill hundreds of thousands of Jews.

"In the result therefore the defence of justification succeeds."

13

The Internet Must Be the New Battleground Against Holocaust Denial

Joe Mulhall

Joe Mulhall received his PhD on postwar fascism from Royal Holloway University of London. He is a senior researcher at the anti-racism organization Hope Not Hate.

For fascism to rise again, Holocaust truths must be downplayed and expunged. Joe Mulhall argues that this is the thinking of those who have wanted to resurrect Nazism since 1945. But such motives are not limited. Holocaust denial extends now into eastern Europe and among Muslims. The new promotional vehicle is the internet, particularly social media platforms and fringe websites. Mulhall issues a call to action to recognize these new forms of denial and to be prepared to combat them in the field of cyberspace.

In 1945, as the news of organised mass murder and gas chambers shocked the world, the far right's dream of a fascist future was left shattered in the ruins of Berlin.

The horrors of the Holocaust became the primary roadblock to the resurrection of fascism's besmirched ideology. Many on the far right believed then, as they do now, that if fascism was ever to rise again then the truth of the Holocaust had to be destroyed.

Since Germany's military defeat in 1945, Holocaust denial has been an attempt by surviving unreconstructed Nazis and their

"Holocaust Denial Is Changing—the Fight Against It Must Change Too," by Joe Mulhall, Guardian News and Media Limited, November 21, 2018. Reprinted by permission.

postwar acolytes to whitewash the monstrous crimes of the Third Reich in the hope of rehabilitating the Nazi regime.

However, denial of the Holocaust has never been a monopoly of the far right. History has taught us that antisemitism arises in many forms, and this is no less true for Holocaust denial. That's why Hope Not Hate's new book also explores denial to be found in leftwing circles, in eastern Europe and from Muslims both in Muslim-majority countries and in the west as well.

Beyond considering contemporary political, religious and geographical dimensions to Holocaust denial, one of the key findings of the book is the worrying generational shift and the changing nature of far-right Holocaust denial engendered by the explosion of the internet.

Recognising the internet's potential for reaching people at an unprecedented scale, Holocaust deniers were early adopters of online platforms, some as early as the 1980s. And since the 2000s social media's arrival has had a profound impact, not just on the ability of the denial community to spread their ideas but more fundamentally on the idea of, and motivation for, Holocaust denial itself.

The good news is that in the past decade there has been a noticeable decline in influence of the traditional Holocaust denial movement, drawn from among a hardcore of far-right believers. The ageing scene has struggled to rejuvenate itself while many of its most prominent activists, such as David Irving, have become less and less active, or unable to fill the venues they once did, while other major figures such as the notorious French academic Robert Faurisson have died.

Even the powerhouse organisations of the denial movement no longer hold the sway they once did. The California-based Institute for Historical Review (IHR), for example, has continued to host conferences but the majority of such events in the west are small or else subsumed into other far-right gatherings, which do not exist to specifically emphasise Holocaust "revisionism."

It has become clear that the traditional far-right Holocaust denial scene, striving towards pseudo-academic respectability amid increasing old age, has (thankfully) failed to attract new members because it has not positioned or organised itself in a way that is accessible and attractive to a younger audience.

However, Holocaust denial—and antisemitism more widely—are far from being in decline. Both are very much present in the modern far right and are central to the international far-right movement known as the alt-right.

For the new generation of online far-right activists that dwell on neo-Nazi websites such as the Daily Stormer or internet image boards such as 4Chan, the pseudo-intellectualism of traditional Holocaust denial is often now eclipsed by a style of deliberately subversive Holocaust "humour." This "for the lulz" attitude is prevalent among the young, online far right. Where once deniers went to great lengths to scientifically "prove" the Holocaust didn't happen, alt-right deniers are more likely to joke about it or even celebrate it.

A 2018 article on the Daily Stormer, for example, is titled: "Germany: British Woman Investigated for Denying Kooky Fake Shower Room Hoax," typifying the casual way in which the alt-right engages with the Holocaust and antisemitism.

Similarly, recognising the changing dynamics of communicating Holocaust denial in the social media age, a thread on the website's forum called "How would you debunk the Holocaust in 140 characters or less?", was started by a user last year.

Another fundamental difference between the nature of the alt-right's denial and the denial of more traditional far-right movements is the lack of importance placed on the Holocaust. For many traditional far-right antisemites, the Holocaust represented the primary obstacle to the resurrection of their fascist creed. However, as a result of the increasing distance from the second world war and the young age of many alt-right activists, some perceive the Holocaust as ancient history.

This view is typified by a number of tweets from the American antisemitic conspiracy theorist and white nationalist Mike Peinovich (aka Mike Enoch), noted for promoting the PizzaGate conspiracy theory, published on the UK's Holocaust Memorial Day in 2018: "Here's the thing Jews. Real or fake, I don't give a f*ck about the holocaust, mmmkay. #HolocaustMemorialDay"

For many young far-right activists the Holocaust is shorn of historical significance, diminished by time and absent from their collective consciousness, as it was not for previous generations throughout the postwar period. Far-right Holocaust denial is changing and if we are to be ready to fight back against those who seek to rewrite history for their own political ends, we have to understand how they are trying to do it.

14

Early Warning Signs of Genocide Are Possible to Detect

Jason Beaubien

Jason Beaubien is the Global Health and Development correspondent for National Public Radio's science desk.

Scholars at the US Holocaust Memorial Museum in Washington, DC, and from Dartmouth College have developed computational tools that can predict possible genocide. Indicators of genocide in this Early Warning Project include local conditions and typical statistics— such as per capita gross domestic product—as well as the form of government. However, Holocaust scholar Greg Stanton believes the Early Warning Project's use of national data—typically a year old when reported—arrives too late to enable useful predictions, which prompted him to create his own prediction system.

History unfortunately does repeat itself.

Two thousand years ago the Romans laid siege to Carthage, killing more than half of the city's residents and enslaving the rest.

Hitler attempted to annihilate the Jews in Europe. In 1994 the Hutus turned on the Tutsis in Rwanda. The Khmer Rouge killed a quarter of Cambodia's population. After the breakup of Yugoslavia,

Serbs slaughtered thousands of Bosnians at Srebrenica in July of 1995.

Last year when Buddhists attacked Rohingya Muslims in Myanmar, many people were shocked to hear that mass killings still occur in the 21st century. But they do—and there's growing evidence that these events follow familiar patterns. And if they do, we should be able to see them coming.

"Genocides are not spontaneous," says Jill Savitt, acting director of the Simon-Skjodt Center for the Prevention of Genocide at the US Holocaust Memorial Museum in Washington, D.C. "In the lead-up to these types of crimes we do see a consistent set of things happening."

Since 2014, the Holocaust Museum and scholars from Dartmouth have mapped the conditions that precede a genocide. They built a database of every mass killing since World War II. Then they went back and looked at the conditions in the countries where the killings occurred just prior to the attacks. And now they use that computer model to analyze which nations currently are at greatest risk.

"We're not forecasting with precision. That's not the intention of the tool," Savitt says. "What we're doing is trying to alert policymakers that here's a situation that is ripe for horrors to happen and give them a heads up that there are actions that can be taken to avert it."

In the three years prior to the attacks on the Rohingya, Myanmar ranked as the country most likely to have a mass killing for two of those years and ranked No. 3 the other year.

The museum's computer model analyzes statistics that you might think have nothing to do with genocide—fluctuations in per capita gross domestic product, infant mortality rates, overall population. Such factors, they believe, are indicators of inequality, poverty and economic instability.

They also plug in data about recent coup attempts, levels of authoritarianism, civil rights, political killings and ethnic polarization.

Lawrence Woocher, the research director at the Simon-Skjodt Center for the Prevention of Genocide at the US Holocaust Museum, has worked on the Early Warning Project since 2014. He says that the form of government is one of the key data points in their computer model. The most dangerous appears to be a regime that's not a full dictatorship but also not a full democracy.

"The prevailing view about why mass atrocities occur is that they tend to be decisions by political elites when they feel under threat and in a condition of instability," Woocher says. "And there's lots of analysis that suggests that these middle regime types are less stable than full democracies or full autocracies."

The Early Warning Project ranks 162 countries by their potential for a new mass killing to erupt in the coming year. They define a "mass killing" as more than 1,000 people being killed by soldiers, a militia or some other armed group. The Democratic Republic of the Congo is currently the most at risk followed by Afghanistan.

Egypt is No. 3 on the list. The researchers note that Egypt was ranked so high because of a variety of factors including a lack of freedom of movement of men, a history of mass killings and a recent coup d'etat. They add that Egypt faces multiple security threats and that "there have been reports of large-scale attacks by extremist groups, including IS [Islamic State], on Christians and Sufi Muslims, and violence against civilians perpetrated by both insurgents and government forces in the Sinai Peninsula."

War-torn South Sudan is No. 4 on the list. Its incredibly brutal civil war is expected to get even worse.

Greg Stanton, a professor at George Mason University and the president of Genocide Watch, agrees with the goal of the Early Warning Project rankings but disagrees with their methods. Stanton says the Holocaust Museum's model is overly dependent on national data that's often released only once a year.

"They tend to notice that there is a risk of genocide too late," Stanton says.

Rather than looking at statistics to try to predict mass killings, he argues that you should look at events.

"In other words, it's not enough to know that you have an authoritarian regime," he says. "It's important to know what that authoritarian regime is doing."

Stanton has come up with a genocide prediction model based on 10 stages of genocide. His model starts with classification of people by ethnicity, race or religion, moves through dehumanization, persecution and extermination before stage 10—denial during and immediately after a genocidal act.

Interestingly, the US currently ticks off many of the early stages of a country headed for a bloodbath, according to Stanton. There's polarization, discrimination, dehumanization. But strong legal and government institutions in the US are likely to block such a disaster from happening, he says.

The information that Genocide Watch and the Holocaust Museum are sifting through has been available to national security agencies for decades. The big question is what to do with this information. At the time of the Rwandan genocide in 1994, Stanton was working in the State Department; he says top government officials knew that the violence was about to begin.

"When President Clinton said after the Rwandan genocide, 'We really didn't know.' I'll be direct. He was lying. He did know," Stanton says. "I've read the confidential cables that came in from Rwanda from our ambassador there months before that genocide. And they knew it was coming."

Stanton's 10 stages of genocide and the Holocaust Museum's Early Warning Project are both attempts to spread information more widely about the early rumblings of a genocide so that world leaders and others might be able to stop it.

15

UN Peacekeepers May Thwart Missions Through Their Own Violence

Nimmi Gowrinathan and Kate Cronin-Furman

Nimmi Gowrinathan is a professor at the Colin Powell School for Civic and Global Leadership, where she is the director of the Politics of Sexual Violence Initiative. Kate Cronin-Furman is a human rights lawyer and political scientist.

Countries in turmoil often rely on the United Nations to bring about and keep the peace. But reports from the Associated Press cited two thousand allegations of sexual abuse by UN personnel from around the world, including those from Sri Lanka who were deployed to Haiti. Nimmi Gowrinathan and Kate Cronin-Furman argue that these peacekeepers are political actors following the agenda of their home country. They contend that peacekeepers are hardly neutral forces, and without punitive actions taken against them, these so-called peacekeepers will continue on their path of violence wherever they go.

Last month's Associated Press (AP) report on the estimated 2,000 allegations of sexual abuse and exploitation by peacekeepers and United Nations personnel around the world wasn't precisely breaking news. Allegations of serious misconduct directed by peacekeeping troops have dogged the UN for years. But the AP report contained several testimonies from the victims of Sri Lankan peacekeepers, who sexually abused and raped children

"UN Peacekeepers: Keeping the Peace or Preventing It?" by Nimmi Gowrinathan and Kate Cronin-Furman, Al Jazeera America, LLC, May 2, 2017. Reprinted by permission.

during the UN Stabilisation Mission in Haiti (MINUSTAH), and these searing testimonies once again highlighted the cost of impunity for sexual violence by UN personnel.

Beyond a blemish on the reputation of the UN, these violations fuel a culture of violence that undermines the potential for sustainable peace.

Within the organisation, sexual violence by peacekeepers is treated with condemnation and, at most, re-location. The UN has no power to prosecute them for their crimes and the Status of Forces agreements (SOFA) that govern UN missions insulate peacekeepers from the criminal jurisdiction of the host country. As a result, the sole responsibility to provide accountability for the crimes of UN peacekeepers rests with their own governments.

In 2007, more than 100 Sri Lankan peacekeeping troops were sent back to their home country from Haiti in disgrace as a result of sexual abuse allegations. The Sri Lankan government promised to investigate and prosecute the guilty but it has not done so. While the Ministry of Defence has stated that 20 members of the contingent were subjected to disciplinary sanctions in 2009, no one has been prosecuted. And Sri Lankan troops have continued to deploy with UN peacekeeping missions in Haiti and elsewhere.

The focus on the appalling failure to prosecute these soldiers for their crimes obscures the fact that the issue is not just criminal violence on an individual level, but rather it emerges from entrenched political cultures that, intentionally, result in a collective failure to protect vulnerable people.

"Conflict-related sexual violence" is a major thematic focus for the UN. Yet, despite clearly qualifying under the requirement that it be "directly or indirectly linked (temporally, geographically or causally) to a conflict," the sexual violence of peacekeepers is rarely understood to be tied to conflict dynamics. But peacekeepers are explicitly political actors.

Impunity Beyond National Borders

While peacekeeping missions are newly created forces, they are made up of national contingents that have been socialised in very particular rules of engagement, rooted in the particular underlying political agendas of their home country.

The Sri Lankan troops that deployed to Haiti were members of a military apparatus that had been fighting a brutal civil war for over two decades and was implicated in widespread and systematic human rights abuses. Arriving in Haiti, the Sri Lankan contingent brought with them a deeply entrenched culture of impunity for crimes against civilians.

Rape, in particular, became endemic as a form of political repression, and reprisal, over the course of the conflict between the Sri Lankan military and the Liberation Tigers of Tamil Eelam (LTTE). It was almost never prosecuted. Despite frequent reports of sexual violence during combat operations, and the routine commission of custodial rape against both women and men, Sri Lankan military personnel have been convicted for exactly one instance of wartime sexual violence: the 1996 gang rape and murder of Tamil schoolgirl Krishanthi Kumaraswamy. The default response of successive Sri Lankan regimes to allegations of military rape, and indeed all state-perpetrated human rights abuses, has been denial and, when pressed, window-dressing inquiries that lead nowhere.

In the final phases of the war in 2009, rights groups reported widespread sexual violence (rape, forced abortions, forced prostitution) of vulnerable populations amongst other alleged war crimes. While a few high-profile cases were covered in the local media, none resulted in convictions. Sri Lankan military forces, from rank and file cadre up to high-level commanders, are guaranteed protection from prosecution.

Carrying with them past crimes and heavy-handed tactics, peacekeepers are hardly the "neutral" incoming forces they are construed as. As they land, they also occupy a particular political space in their host country. Their function is to ensure stability and prevent the resurgence of violence; necessarily a status quo enforcing role. They are therefore tied, especially in the minds of aggrieved or marginalised populations, to the state's political agenda. This means that the violence of peacekeepers is, in some senses, the violence of the state.

Extreme Marginilisation

Like Sri Lanka, Haiti's civil strife over the past three decades has been marked by state-sanctioned rape, forced disappearances, and massacres of civilians—largely to quell political dissent and resistance. MINUSTAH bases, like those the Haitian children were reported as being forced into, are carefully placed in neighbourhoods whose residents have lived their entire lives under the shadow of state violence. To civilians in this area, rape at the hands of armed men is inevitable. In 2007, a Haitian woman interviewed confirmed the depth of this militarised culture of violence. "(There is) no difference between the police and the gangs. They all have guns and they can do whatever they want," she said.

State-perpetrated sexual violence places all its victims, but particularly women, in positions of extreme marginalisation. These victims often find themselves ostracised by their communities and at an increased risk of retribution by military forces. An under-recognised result of this violence is its impact on women's political perceptions in ways that encourage identification with extremist, or violent, political movements.

In Haiti, before the arrival of the peacekeepers, the prevalence of rape had already created an urgent need for self-protection, and a deep disillusionment with the state, leading to a significant increase in women joining the armed gangs and vigilante groups driving pervasive violence. The sexual violence of peacekeepers, tied to both the protection failures and the violence of the state, has only exacerbated these dynamics. Rape by state military forces, as a political act, will always have a political impact. Rape by UN peacekeepers, often the last resort for protection, will leave in its wake even more willing recruits for armed groups.

If peacekeepers carry their politics with them to their host country, they don't leave them there. As successive waves of Sri Lankan peacekeepers have returned home from Haiti, they have re-engaged in the ethnic conflict; first in combat roles, and then, following the end of the war in 2009, as part of the occupying force in northeast Sri Lanka. Several of the peacekeeping contingent's leadership went on to positions of high authority in the Sri Lankan military, including brigade and division commander, and director of military intelligence.

These individuals have presided over a heavily militarised former conflict zone in which rape and sexual exploitation of vulnerable Tamil women, similar to that inflicted on the Haitian population, have been common. This violence undermines prospects for a lasting peace. From our post-conflict research in Sri Lanka, several interviewees noted that, "when people in the community think of the situation now of Tamil women, they think we have to resurrect the LTTE."

Driving a Resurgence of Violence

Just a few weeks before the Sri Lankan troops were sent home in 2007, the contingent's former second-in-command, Colonel Mahinda Weerasooriya, told a domestic newspaper that by participating in UN peacekeeping operations: "We have proven that the Sri Lankan army is not an army that violates human rights and we have proven that we are a well-disciplined army."

Yet, if Sri Lanka's participation in UN peacekeeping has proven anything, it is that abusive military cultures survive transplantation to new environments. Soldiers who exploit and abuse vulnerable populations at home will do so abroad as well—undermining the prospects for peace in both spaces. Peacekeeper violence has political impacts far beyond the creation of new victims.

While it is incontrovertible that peacekeepers who abuse civilian populations should be prosecuted for their crimes, these individual trials are not enough. Peacekeeper violence should be treated with the same seriousness as other types of conflict-related sexual violence. National contingents should be more thoroughly vetted before deployment, and stronger monitoring and disciplinary sanctions should be imposed to prevent and punish violations on the ground. Without these comprehensive measures, UN peacekeeping forces will not only fail in their mission to create the conditions for lasting peace, they will be one of the driving forces behind a resurgence of violence—wherever they go.

16

To Effectively Address Genocides, International Law Must Be Decolonized

Frédéric Mégret

Frédéric Mégret is a professor at McGill University in Montreal. His research focuses on international law, human rights, the laws of war, and criminal justice.

The National Inquiry into Missing and Murdered Indigenous Women and Girls (MMIWG) commission in Canada reflects the ways in which international law is itself a colonial construct. Historically, colonial massacres have not been considered genocides or crimes against humanity by the UN genocide convention, which instead strictly focuses on large-scale massacres like the Holocaust and Rwandan genocide. Gendered and indigenous groups are not considered protected populations by the UN convention. Through acknowledging that colonial genocide is distinct from Holocaust-style genocide—but just as insidious and damaging—the MMIWG is working to correct this gap in international law.

The National Inquiry into Missing and Murdered Indigenous Women and Girls (MMIWG) has come to the conclusion that Canada has committed genocide against its Indigenous peoples. This is buttressed by a dense and sophisticated 46-page supplementary legal analysis appended to the report.

"The MMIWG Report: A Call for Decolonizing International Law Itself," by Frédéric Mégret, The Conversation, June 9, 2019, https://theconversation.com/the-mmiwg-report-a-call-for-decolonizing-international-law-itself-118443. Licensed under CC BY-ND 4.0 International.

International lawyers hardly have a monopoly over what is or ought to be characterized as genocide—the issue is also the subject of debate among historians, social scientists and the general public. Nonetheless, genocide as a legal term was the creation of international law. The recognition that it happened is legally significant.

The supplementary legal analysis is careful to emphasize that it cannot be the last word on the matter, but it does come up with a series of strong arguments that draw upon international law.

The United Nations' Genocide Convention must be interpreted in the light of evolving customary international law: states can be liable for genocide as well as individuals; one can commit genocide through omissions as well as actions; responsibility can be incurred for ongoing and disparate acts; members of a group can be killed in a variety of ways.

In my opinion, some international lawyers who might otherwise be sympathetic to the plight of Indigenous groups in Canada could nonetheless hesitate to label what happened as genocide.

They may emphasize, for example, the non-applicability of the Genocide Convention for much of the period during which it was allegedly violated in Canada. They may argue that only physical and biological killing of the group is covered by the convention. Or they may point out that Indigenous groups were purportedly not covered by the provisions of the Genocide Convention. They may opine that simply because something is not classified as genocide doesn't mean it's not despicable or worthy of condemnation.

Missing the Point

Such hesitations are understandable, but they miss the larger point.

The attempt to grapple with genocide in Canada by the MMIWG commission is about more than simply applying international law to the facts. It's also about decolonizing the international law of genocide itself; that is, imagining what international law could be if it had not itself been implicated historically in colonization.

Just as it draws on the authority of international law, the MMIWG report is also a subtle indictment of it.

International law defined genocide narrowly after the Second World War and largely reflected the unique experience of the Holocaust. Colonial massacres before then—such as the genocide of the Herero in southern Africa—or even at the time, like the Sétif massacre in Algeria, were not considered genocide or crimes against humanity.

The focus on individual criminal responsibility in the last two decades may have further reinforced a sense that genocide is committed by a few "bad apples."

A determination of genocide in Canada, therefore, is partly *despite* the UN genocide convention's failure to include Indigenous or gendered groups as protected minorities, its emphasis on massacres and its insistence on individual intent.

The convention makes it structurally difficult to conceptualize genocide as being anything other than the sort of industrial killing or large-scale massacre illustrated by the Holocaust and the Rwandan genocide respectively.

But if we accept that international law—which, by the way, historically sanctified colonization—is not a sacred source of authority but part of a particular, historically and geographically situated tradition, then we can begin to imagine how we might rethink genocide.

Decolonizing Genocide

The MMIWG report suggests, in particular, that we ought to think of "colonial genocide" as different from "Holocaust genocide." It is a genocide happening everywhere and all the time. It is a genocide that is at least as much the result of a slow war of cultural attrition than it is the product of massacres. The intent is present but it is structural. Responsibility is not only singular, not the work of a few bad apples, but collective.

Paradoxically, then, the challenge is not only to denounce a genocide but to denounce the limitations of the international law on genocide.

It is to question the authority to define "genocide" and to foreground victims' experience in defining it. It is to insist that colonial genocide is genocide too. It is to recognize what happened in Canada over several centuries for what it is, despite the law's best efforts to beat around the bush.

To decolonize genocide, then, is to decolonize how we comprehend genocide and to reimagine what international law could stand for.

There has been much debate since the MMIWG report's release about what its legal consequences will be. The Organization of American States has asked Canada to agree to the creation of a panel to further investigate the allegation of genocide.

This is helpful because it places the struggle for Indigenous rights within the broader scope of solidarity within the Americas. But the main lesson of the report may be more introspective and one that requires a slow reckoning with its analysis.

In the end, the conclusion of the MMIWG inquiry reflects the difficulty of, as the American writer Audre Lorde once put it, "dismantling the master's house with the master's tools."

But in attempting to dismantle that house, the report makes it clear that the obligation to address genocide is, through and through, an obligation to decolonize.

17

Ordinary People Can Perpetrate Genocides

University of New Hampshire Tales

The University of New Hampshire Tales blog allows university students and alumni of the university to share news and opinions.

This viewpoint discusses the findings of Dr. James Waller, a professor of Holocaust and genocide studies who wrote the book Becoming Evil: How Ordinary People Commit Genocide and Mass Murder *and presented a lecture at the University of New Hampshire on this topic. Dr. Waller's work focuses on the perpetrators of genocides, a number of whom he interviewed to gain insight into their emotions and motivations when committing these acts. His findings are both surprising and disturbing: Most of the perpetrators are ordinary people who were simply encouraged to kill through group dynamics and managed to reconfigure their mindsets to justify these acts.*

The cold and rainy weather didn't stop students from making their way to the MUB Theater I for Dr. James Waller's lecture. Dr. James Waller, a Cohen Professor of Holocaust and Genocide Studies at Keene State College in New Hampshire was speaking about themes from his book, *Becoming Evil: How Ordinary People Commit Genocide and Mass Killing.* When I first saw posters for this event I was immediately intrigued by such a topic. I wasn't the only one either; at 7:55 with only 5 minutes

"Becoming Evil: How Ordinary People Commit Genocide and Mass Killing—Guest Lecture," *University of New Hampshire Tales*, University of New Hampshire, May 2, 2014. Reprinted by permission.

before Dr. Waller took the podium, the theater was full with no standing room left.

Dr. Waller was introduced by his daughter, Hannah Waller, a UNH student. He immediately began talking about the history of genocide and mass killings. Included in this portion of the lecture was a shocking statistic—in the 20th century alone, it is estimated that 60 million people lost their lives due to genocides or mass killings. What's even crazier is that Dr. Waller believes that is a conservative number.

"How many people did it take to kill 6 million people?" Dr. Waller, referring to the Holocaust, asked the room. There was silence. No one, not even Dr. Waller had an answer but what was interesting, is that the question was one that I hadn't ever thought about. We focus on the victims, not the perpetrators, except when speaking of the evil that was done by them. The core of Dr. Waller's lecture was perpetrators and how they are enlisted to perpetrate such evils.

The choices perpetrators faced, the emotions they felt, the coping mechanisms they used, and the changes they underwent, were all things that Dr. Waller's work focuses on. He has interviewed both perpetrators and survivors to try and get some answers to those statements. The problem with this, however, is while speaking to the perpetrators, one may start to feel a sense of empathy towards them. The point of the lecture was not to feel empathetic, but to understand how the perpetrators of genocide and mass killings came to kill, as Dr. Waller pointed out.

Many people, including myself, would like to believe that perpetrators of such crimes are the complete opposite of us. Dr. Waller pointed out that, "it is ordinary people, like you and me, who commit genocide and mass killings." This statement shifted the energy in the room. He went on to explain that while interviewing perpetrators, he is struck by how ordinary the perpetrators' lives are outside of their "job" of killing each day.

Dr. Waller gave the example of the first set of Nuremburg trials. 21 men were tried and both IQ and personality tests were administered in attempts to try and prove these perpetrators had a "Nazi personality" (or some part of their personality that made them commit such atrocities). Scores from both tests came back and showcd nothing out of thc ordinary for all but a man named Julius Streicher. The other 20 men allegedly didn't want to be tried with Streicher because they said he was "crazy." "When a Nazi says you're crazy, you're pretty far gone," joked Dr. Waller. This example illustrated to the audience that even Nazis (with the exception of Streicher) didn't have something distinct about their personality that would explain their behavior during the Holocaust.

At this point I was wondering, as I'm sure many others were, what causes this behavior? I've read numerous works of nonfiction crime and many have cited certain psychological studies to back up the behavior of the crimes discussed. However, Dr. Waller explained that what makes perpetrators of genocide and mass killing different is the group dynamic. Any type of group amplifies a situation, either for bad or for good, Dr. Waller explained. Individual killers in these groups believe that killing itself is wrong but it is a worse wrong to not kill. That subtle difference may be the key element in what separates the mentality of "them" and "us." Dr. Waller also pointed out that perpetrators have a very high sense of morality BUT their morality goes in the opposite direction of ours. For the perpetrator, the victim means nothing to them morally speaking, but for us, we will empathize for the victim and with the victim's loved ones. Perpetrators are able to reconfigure their mindsets, justifying their actions.

Before opening the floor for questions, Dr. James Waller ended with the Arthur Ashe quote, "Start where you are. Use what you have. Do what you can." Stopping genocide and mass killings may seem like an overwhelming task, but Dr. Waller urged the audience to follow the wise words of Arthur Ashe. This quote was an inspiring end to an extremely interesting lecture.

18

Surviving Genocide in Colonial Namibia

Heicke Becker

Heicke Becker is a professor of anthropology at the University of the Western Cape in South Africa. Her research focuses on the connections of politics and aesthetics, popular culture, social movements, popular protests, and nationalism.

Though many people think of the Holocaust as the first example of genocide, other instances of genocide occurred well before then. This includes the genocide committed by Germany between 1904 and 1905 in what is now known as Namibia, but was then called German South West Africa. Large percentages of the Ovaherero and Nama people died of starvation, thirst, overwork, and exposure at the hands of the Germans, and many consider this early act of genocide the template for the Holocaust. This viewpoint discussess the book Mama Penee: Transcending the Genocide, *which examines the genocide on a personal level through the eyes of an eleven-year-old and shows the human impact of these events.*

Germany committed genocide in Africa 40 years before the Holocaust of the European Jews. In 1904 and 1905 the Ovaherero and Nama people of central and southern Namibia rose up against colonial rule and dispossession in what was then called German South West Africa. The revolt was brutally crushed.

"Surviving Genocide: A Voice from Colonial Namibia at the Turn of the Last Century," by Heicke Becker, The Conversation, January 26, 2020, https://theconversation. com/surviving-genocide-a-voice-from-colonial-namibia-at-the-turn-of-the-last-century-130546. Licensed under CC BY-ND 4.0 International.

By 1908, 80% of the Ovaherero and 50% of the Nama had died of starvation and thirst, overwork and exposure to harsh climates.

The army drove survivors into the waterless Omaheke desert. Thousands more died in concentration camps.

For many historians this first genocide committed by Germany provided the template for the horrors that were to come 40 years later during the Holocaust of the European Jews. The philosopher Hannah Arendt, herself a Holocaust refugee from Germany, explained in 1951 that European imperialism played a crucial role in the development of Nazi totalitarianism and associated genocides.

We know very little about the experience of those who lived through this first systematic mass extinction of the 20th century. Forty-seven testimonies were recorded and published in 1918 in a scathing official British report about German colonial rule in Namibia, known as the Blue Book. One eyewitness remarked: "Words cannot be found to relate what happened; it was too terrible."

Following on an earlier Norwegian edition, a new book, *Mama Penee: Transcending the Genocide*, by Uazuvara Ewald Kapombo Katjivena, to be published by UNAM Press in Windhoek in February, makes an extraordinary attempt to present the lived experience of the genocide.

Surviving a Genocide

Based on oral and family history, Katjivena, a former exiled liberation Namibian fighter until the country's independence from South Africa in 1990, tells his grandmother's story in a biography deeply infused with family and oral history. His grandmother, Jahohora, survived the genocide as an 11-year-old girl.

In the book's opening scene young Jahohora witnesses her parents' murder at the hands of German colonial troops in 1904. Following this traumatic experience, she wanders into the veld. The young girl survives on her own, using skills that her mother had imparted to her, to scavenge from the environment. She traps rabbits and birds, eats berries and wild honey, and occasionally feasts on an ostrich egg.

The remaining connection with her parents is cruelly cut after she is caught and forced to work for a German farmer. During the "civilising" washing and changing of her attire, her ceremonial Ovaherero headgear is cut into pieces and burnt by the farmer's wife.

The headgear was her mother's significant gift for the growing daughter just before the start of the hostilities in early 1904. Jahohora suffers deeply humiliating experiences.

Katjivena's grandmother was a remarkable woman of deep thought, insight, and immense resolve. Her parents and grandparents belonged to a section of the Ovaherero called the Ovatjurure. They played a significant role in their communities by helping to maintain peace among families in the nearby homesteads and in the neighbouring villages.

Their daughter passed on this remarkable tradition to the children and grandchildren she brought up during Namibia's colonial era under Germany and South Africa.

Regaining Agency

Katjivena intersperses Jahohora's personal perspective with historical facts. We read a detailed, chilling account of General Lothar von Trotha's extermination order of 2 October 1904. The oral history telling, however, also indicates instances of humanity during an entirely inhumane era.

Who were these white people, the survivor wondered. Why had some German soldiers saved her from certain death and given her a chance of life while their fellows had mercilessly killed her parents? As Jahohora meets other survivors and hears their stories, she begins to understand the genocide and especially the role of Von Trotha, who is locally known as omuzepe (the killer).

Katjivena's story looks simple, yet it exudes deep meaning. It turns the gaze onto the oppressors. The resisting gaze of the colonised, the cultural theorist Elizabeth Baer writes, is an act of self-creation. It "begins to recognize and restore agency to the victims of imperialism."

Transcending the Genocide

The subtitle of Katjivena's book is Transcending the Genocide. It adds a tremendous living voice to the symbolic commemorations of Germany's African genocide that have taken place over the past few years.

Importantly, human remains of genocide victims were repatriated from Germany to Namibia in 2011, 2014 and 2018. These had been shipped to academic and medical institutions in Germany, and had remained there until recently.

In 2019 some significant items of cultural memory, which had been stolen during colonial conquest, were returned to Namibia from the Linden Museum in Stuttgart. These included the slain Nama leader Hendrik Witbooi's Bible and his riding whip.

In Windhoek a Genocide Memorial, built in 2014, signifies a noteworthy shift in post-colonial Namibian memory politics. The statue's North Korean aesthetics and symbolism remain controversial. That aside, the new monument shows that the genocide of the Ovaherero and Nama has belatedly entered the public history narrative of Namibian nationhood. This would have been impossible a few years earlier.

Reconciliation and Reparations

On the political level, the German government finally acknowledged the colonial genocide in 2015. Ever since, Namibian and German envoys have been talking about an official apology by Germany.

Most controversial have been negotiations about reparations. Also controversial has been the role of the Ovaherero and Nama communities that were directly affected by the genocide. But in January 2020 Germany's new ambassador to Namibia, Herbert Beck, hinted that important political developments might be about to happen.

It is not clear yet where the complicated process of post-colonial reconciliation is going. Yet, with stories such as Katjivena's remarkable biography of his grandmother, the dead and the survivors of the colonial genocide are finally given a face.

19

The United States Is Complicit in the Saudi-Led Genocide in Yemen

Jeff Bachman

Jeff Bachman is a professorial lecturer in human rights and the director of the Ethics, Peace, and Human Rights MA program at the American University School of International Service in Washington, DC.

Yemen has been involved in a civil war since 2015 between the Shia Houthi movement and the government, which is backed by Sunni Saudi Arabia. Because of its investment in the conflict, Saudi Arabia has been directly involved in attacks against the Houthis, and the US—as an ally of Saudi Arabia—has supported the efforts. However, this conflict has gone beyond military engagement to what Jeff Bachman describes as genocide. Many of the bombing attacks have been on civilians, and an air and naval blockade has caused millions of people to go without food and medical aid for treatable diseases and injuries. According to the author, this humanitarian crisis must be acknowledged as an act of genocide, and the US must take responsibility for its part in it.

A Saudi-led coalition of states has been aggressively bombing Yemen and imposing an air and naval blockade of its ports for more than three years, leading UN Secretary General

"US Complicity in the Saudi-led Genocide in Yemen Spans Obama and Trump Administrations," by Jeff Bachman, The Conversation, November 26, 2018, https://theconversation.com/us-complicity-in-the-saudi-led-genocide-in-yemen-spans-obama-trump-administrations-106896. Licensed under CC BY-ND 4.0 International.

Antonio Guterres to describe Yemen as "the world's worst humanitarian crisis."

Guterres put the crisis in stark perspective, emphasizing the near complete lack of security for the Yemeni people. More than 22 million people out of a total population of 28 million are in need of humanitarian aid and protection. Eighteen million people lack reliable access to food; 8.4 million people "do not know how they will obtain their next meal."

As a scholar of genocide and human rights, I believe the destruction brought about by these attacks combined with the blockade amounts to genocide.

Based on my research, to be published in an upcoming issue of Third World Quarterly, I believe the coalition would not be capable of committing this crime without the material and logistical support of both the Obama and Trump administrations.

A 'Storm' Recast as 'Hope'

Yemen has been gripped by a civil war since 2015, pitting the Shia Houthi movement—which has fought for centuries for control of parts of Yemen—against a government backed by Sunni Saudi Arabia. Because of these religious differences, it would be easy to recast what is largely a political conflict in Yemen as a sectarian one.

That characterization fits Saudi and US assertions that the Houthis are controlled by Shiite Iran, a claim that has not gone uncontested. Both the Saudis and the US are hostile to Iran, so US support of Saudi Arabia in Yemen represents what US administrations have said are strategic interests in the region.

Besides Saudi Arabia, the coalition attacking Yemen includes the United Arab Emirates, Egypt, Morocco, Jordan, Sudan, Kuwait and Bahrain. Qatar was part of the coalition but is no longer.

During the first three years of "Operation Decisive Storm," later renamed "Operation Renewal of Hope," 16,749 coalition air attacks in Yemen were documented by the Yemen Data Project (YDP), which describes itself as an "independent data collection project aimed at collecting and disseminating data on the conduct of the war in Yemen."

Based on the information available to it using open sources, YDP reports that two-thirds of the coalition's bombing attacks have been against non-military and unknown targets. The coalition isn't accidentally attacking civilians and civilian infrastructure—it's doing it deliberately.

That's evident from the kind—and volume—of civilian targets documented. They include places that are generally protected against attack even under the lax rules of international humanitarian law: Residential areas, vehicles, marketplaces and mosques as well as boats, social gatherings and camps for internally displaced persons.

Because of the role it plays in movement of people, food and medicine, Yemen's transportation infrastructure is especially important. Airports, ports, bridges and roads have all been repeatedly attacked.

Yemen's economic infrastructure—farms, private businesses and factories, oil and gas facilities, water and electricity lines and food storage—have also been hit. And the coalition has targeted and destroyed schools and medical facilities, too.

Finally, Yemen's cultural heritage has been attacked. In all, at least 78 cultural sites have been damaged or destroyed, including archaeological sites, museums, mosques, churches and tombs, as well as numerous other monuments and residences that have great historical and cultural significance.

How to Make a Crisis

The attacks aren't the only way the coalition is creating a massive humanitarian crisis.

The air and naval blockade, in effect since March 2015, "is essentially using the threat of starvation as a bargaining tool and an instrument of war," according to the UN panel of experts on Yemen.

The blockade stops and inspects vessels seeking entry to Yemen's ports. That allows the coalition to regulate and restrict Yemenis' access to food, fuel, medical supplies and humanitarian aid.

In his analysis of the blockade's legality, Dutch military scholar Martin Fink writes that the blockade means "massive time delays and uncertainty on what products would be allowed to enter."

Despite UN efforts to alleviate some of the worst delays, imports are often held up for a long time. In some cases, food that makes it through the blockade has already spoiled, if entry is not denied altogether.

In some ways, the humanitarian crisis in Yemen is unprecedented and can be tied directly to the conflict. As the World Bank notes, "Yemen's very difficult economic challenges before the current conflict cannot be compared to the intensely critical situation the country is facing today."

Similarly, Tufts University scholar Alex de Waal describes Yemen as "the greatest famine atrocity of our lifetimes." It was caused, writes de Waal, by the coalition "deliberately destroying the country's food-producing infrastructure."

The failing security for the people of Yemen has been compounded by a failing health system. The World Health Organization reported in September 2017 that only 45 percent of health facilities in Yemen were functional.

As Secretary-General Guterres put it, "Treatable illnesses become a death sentence when local health services are suspended and it is impossible to travel outside the country."

As of February 2018, according to the Office of the High Commissioner for Human Rights, the coalition had killed 6,000 people in airstrikes and wounded nearly 10,000 more.

Yet, according to the OHCHR report, these counts are conservative. Tens of thousands of Yemenis have also died from causes related to the war. According to Save the Children, an estimated 85,000 children under five may have died since 2015, with more than 50,000 child deaths in 2017 alone from hunger and related causes.

Coalition actions in Yemen amount to nothing short of what Raphael Lemkin, the individual who coined the term "genocide," referred to as a "synchronized attack on different aspects of life."

The US Contribution

The coalition's genocide in Yemen would not be possible without the complicity of the US. This has been a bipartisan presidential effort, covering both the Obama and Trump administrations.

US arms are being used to kill Yemenis and destroy their country. In 2016, well after the coalition began its genocidal assault on Yemen, four of the top five recipients of US arms sales were members of the coalition.

The US has also provided the coalition with logistical support, including mid-air refueling, targeting advice and support, intelligence, expedited munitions resupply and maintenance.

Other than the sale of arms, perhaps the most significant contribution to the coalition's ability to commit genocide in Yemen has been the provision of fuel and mid-air refueling of Coalition warplanes, which was halted in early November, 2018. By the middle of 2017, the US had delivered over 67 million pounds of fuel to the coalition and refueled coalition aircraft more than 9,000 times.

Shared Responsibility for Genocide

As a genocide scholar, I believe that under international law, the US shares responsibility with the Coalition for genocide in Yemen.

What does this mean? It means that the US must cease and desist all activities that facilitate genocide in Yemen. This would include stopping all sales of weapons and ending logistical support for Coalition action.

In an ideal world, one in which all states are equally subjects before international law, the US would also seek an advisory opinion from the International Court of Justice regarding what restitution it owes the people of Yemen for its role in the coalition's genocide.

Similarly, the US would request an International Criminal Court investigation into individual culpability of US officials in both the Obama and Trump administrations for their role in facilitating the crimes committed in Yemen.

Of course, this is not an ideal world.

The US recognizes neither the International Court of Justice's authority to judge the legality of its actions, nor the International Criminal Court's authority to investigate the suspected criminal acts of individual US officials. Such an investigation could be triggered by a UN Security Council referral, but the US would simply veto any such effort.

All that is left, then, is for the people of the US to hold their own to account for the crimes committed in their names.

Organizations to Contact

The editors have compiled the following list of organizations concerned with the issues debated in this book. The descriptions are derived from materials provided by the organizations. All have publications or information available for interested readers. The list was compiled on the date of publication of the present volume; the information provided here may change. Be aware that many organizations take several weeks or longer to respond to inquiries, so allow as much time as possible.

Center for the Study of Genocide and Human Rights
Rutgers University
30 College Avenue
New Brunswick, NJ 08901
email: cghr@rutgers.edu
website: global.rutgers.edu/cghr

The Center for the Study of Genocide and Human Rights has a mission to understand and prevent genocide and mass atrocity crimes. Using a critical prevention approach, it analyzes issues and assumptions to offer innovative ideas and solutions.

Facing History and Ourselves
16 Hurd Road
Brookline, MA 02445
website: www.facinghistory.org

Facing History and Ourselves is an organization that partners with educators around the world. It reaches millions of students in thousands of classrooms each year, helping new generations to stand up to hatred and bigotry.

Institute for the Study of Genocide
email: info@instituteforthestudyofgenocide.org
website: www.instituteforthestudyofgenocide.org

The Institute for the Study of Genocide is an independent nonprofit organization that promotes and distributes research and policy analysis on the causes, consequences, and prevention of genocide. It was established in 1982.

International Association of Genocide Scholars
email: info@genocidescholars.org
website: www.genocidescholars.org

The International Association of Genocide Scholars is an interdisciplinary group of specialists who work to advance research and teaching about the causes and ramifications of genocide. Founded in 1994, the association publishes the latest research and promotes policy studies on genocide prevention.

International Criminal Court (ICC)
Oude Waalsdorperweg 10
2587 AK The Hague
The Netherlands
phone: +31 (0) 70 515 8515
email: otp.informationdesk@icc-cpi.int
website; www.icc-cpi.int

The International Criminal Court investigates and prosecutes people charged with genocide, war crimes, crimes against humanity, and the crime of aggression. The ICC works to incorporate and protect victims' voices and to conduct fair trials.

International Crisis Group
149 Avenue Louise
Level 24
B-1050 Brussels
Belgium
phone: +32-2-502-90-38
email: brussels@crisisgroup.org
website: www.crisisgroup.org

The International Crisis Group was founded in 1995 as an international nongovernmental organization focused on genocide prevention. It is now a leading global independent source of analysis and advice to governments and intergovernmental groups, including the United Nations, European Union, and World Bank.

United Nations Office on Genocide Prevention and the Responsibility to Protect
United Nations Secretariat Building
405 E. 42nd Street
New York, NY 10017
phone: (917) 367-2580
email: osapg@un.org
website: www.un.org/en/genocideprevention/

The United Nations Office on Genocide Prevention and the Responsibility to Protect has two Special Advisers. The Special Adviser on the Prevention of Genocide serves as a catalyst to raise awareness of genocide's causes and its dynamics. When risk of genocide occurs, he or she issues alerts and mobilizes action.

United States Holocaust Memorial Museum
100 Raoul Wallenberg Place SW
Washington, DC 20024-2126
phone: (202) 488-0400
website: www.ushmm.org

The United States Holocaust Memorial Museum is a central repository and institution of the US federal government that is intended to warn and educate about the Holocaust and other genocides. It offers programs for scholars, survivors, educators, and students. Its Simon-Skjodt Center for the Prevention of Genocide seeks to take the action that was not available to victims of the Holocaust.

Yad Vashem—The World Holocaust Remembrance Center
Har Hazikaron
POB 3477
Jerusalem 9103401
Israel
phone: 972-2-6443400
email: generalinformation@yadvashem.org.il
website: www.yadvashem.org

Yad Vashem is a central and authoritative source for Holocaust education, documentation, and research. It offers a wide variety of programs and exhibits, and it recognizes "Righteous Among the Nations," rescuers who put their lives at risk to help others during the Holocaust.

Zoryan Institute for Contemporary Armenian Research and Documentation—International Institute for Genocide and Human Rights Studies
255 Duncan Mill Road, Suite 310
Toronto, ON M3B 2H9
Canada
phone: (416) 250-9807
email: zoryan@zoryaninstitute.org
website: www.zoryaninstitute.org

The Zoryan Institute is a nonprofit organization that researches and raises awareness of issues relating to universal human rights and genocide. It runs programs and seminars and issues publications to meet these goals.

Bibliography

Books

Christopher R. Browning. *Ordinary Men: Reserve Police Battalion 101 and the Final Solution in Poland.* New York, NY: HarperPerennial, 2017.

Saul Friedländer. *Nazi Germany and the Jews, Volume I: The Years of Persecution, 1933–1939.* New York, NY: HarperPerennial, 1998.

Saul Friedländer. *Nazi Germany and the Jews, Volume II: The Years of Extermination, 1939–1945.* New York, NY: HarperPerennial, 2007.

Robert Gellately and Ben Kiernan, eds. *The Specter of Genocide: Mass Murder in Historical Perspective.* New York, NY: Cambridge University Press, 2003.

Daniel Jonah Goldhagen. *Hitler's Willing Executioners: Ordinary Germans and the Holocaust.* New York, NY: First Vintage Books/Random House, 1997.

Peter Hayes, ed. *How Was It Possible: A Holocaust Reader.* Lincoln, NE: University of Nebraska Press, 2015.

Raul Hilberg. *Perpetrators Victims Bystanders: The Jewish Catastrophe, 1933–1945.* New York, NY: HarperPerennial, 1993.

Alexander Laban Hinton, ed. *Genocide: An Anthropological Reader.* Malden, MA: Blackwell, 2002.

Alexander Laban Hinton. *Why Did They Kill? Cambodia in the Shadow of Genocide.* Berkeley, CA: University of California Press, 2005.

Alexander Laban Hinton, Thomas LaPointe, and Douglas Irvin-Erickson, eds. *Hidden Genocides: Power, Knowledge, Memory.* New Brunswick, NJ: Rutgers University Press, 2014.

Adam Jones. *Genocide: A Comprehensive Introduction, 3rd Edition.* New York, NY: Routledge, 2017.

Ben Kiernan. *Blood and Soil: A World History of Extermination from Sparta to Darfur.* New Haven, CT: Yale University Press, 2007.

Raphael Lemkin. *Axis Rule in Occupied Europe: Laws of Occupation, Analysis of Government, Proposals for Redress.* Clark, NJ: Law Book Exchange, 2014.

Mark Levene. *Genocide in the Age of the Nation-State, Volume 1: The Meaning of Genocide.* New York, NY: I. B. Tauris & Co., 2005.

Mark Levene. *Genocide in the Age of the Nation-State, Volume 2: The Rise of the West and the Coming of Genocide.* New York, NY: I. B. Tauris & Co., 2005.

Samantha Power. *"Problem from Hell": America in the Age of Genocide.* New York, NY: Basic Books, 2013.

Timothy Snyder. *Bloodlands: Europe Between Hitler and Stalin.* New York, NY: Basic Books, 2010.

Scott Straus. *Fundamentals of Genocide and Mass Atrocity Prevention.* Washington, DC: US Holocaust Memorial Museum, 2014.

Samuel Totten and Paul R. Bartrop, eds. *The Genocide Studies Reader.* New York, NY: Routledge, 2009.

James E. Waller. *Becoming Evil: How Ordinary People Commit Genocide and Mass Killing, 2nd Edition.* New York, NY: Oxford University Press, 2007.

Periodicals and Internet Sources

Colette Bennett, "Elie Wiesel's Speech for Holocaust Units," *ThoughtCo*, May 30, 2019, www.thoughtco.com/perils-of-indifference-for-holocaust-units-3984022.

Claudia Card, "Genocide and Social Death," *Hypatia,* 2003, https://onlinelibrary.wiley.com/doi/abs/10.1111/j.1527-2001.2003.tb00779.x.

Vahakn N. Dadrian, "Children as Victims of Genocide: The Armenian Case," *Journal of Genocide Research,* 2003, https://www.tandfonline.com/doi/abs/10.1080/1462352032000154642?journalCode=cjgr20.

Susan Davis and Tim Mak, "House Rebukes Turkey with Votes on Sanctions, Armenian Genocide," NPR, October 29, 2019, www.npr.org/2019/10/29/774091935/house-seeks-to-rebuke-turkey-with-vote-on-armenian-genocide.

Lee Feinstein and Tod Lindberg, "Finding a Place for Atrocity Prevention Amid New Security Challenges," US Holocaust Memorial Museum, March 22, 2015, www.ushmm.org/genocide-prevention/blog/finding-a-place-for-atrocity-prevention-amid-new-security-challenges.

Daniel A. Gross, "A Brutal Genocide in Colonial Africa Finally Gets Its Deserved Recognition," *Smithsonian Magazine*, October 28, 2015, www.smithsonianmag.com/history/brutal-genocide-colonial-africa-finally-gets-its-deserved-recognition-180957073/.

Shmuel Lederman, "A Nation Destroyed: An Existential Approach to the Distinctive Harm of Genocide," *Journal of Genocide Research*, November 8, 2016, https://www.tandfonline.com/doi/abs/10.1080/14623528.2016.1250473.

Benjamin Madley, "Reexamining the American Genocide Debate: Meaning, Historiography, and New Methods," *American Historical Review*, February 2015, https://academic.oup.com/ahr/article-abstract/120/1/98/47185?redirectedFrom=PDF.

Jackie Northam, "Reporter's Notebook: Rwandan's Trial Triggers Memories of Genocide," NPR, April 9, 2019, www.npr.org/2019/04/09/711341821/reporters-notebook-rwandan-s-trial-triggers-memories-of-genocide.

Christopher Powell, "What Do Genocides Kill? A Relational Conception of Genocide," *Journal of Genocide Research,* November 9, 2007, https://www.tandfonline.com/doi/abs/10.1080/14623520701643285.

Jennifer Rosenberg, "A Short History of the Rwandan Genocide," *ThoughtCo*, May 7, 2019, https://www.thoughtco.com/the-rwandan-genocide-1779931.

Dan Stone, "Genocide as Transgression." *European Journal of Social Theory*, February 1, 2004, https://journals.sagepub.com/doi/10.1177/1368431004040019.

Uğur Ümit Üngör, "Seeing Like a Nation-State: Young Turk Social Engineering in Eastern Turkey, 1913-50," *Journal of Genocide Research*, June 19, 2008, https://www.tandfonline.com/doi/abs/10.1080/14623520701850278.

US Holocaust Memorial Museum, "Cambodia," www.ushmm.org/genocide-prevention/countries/cambodia.

US Holocaust Memorial Museum, "Holocaust Encyclopedia," encyclopedia.ushmm.org.

Robert Wilde, "The Wars of the Former Yugoslavia," *ThoughtCo*, January 15, 2019, www.thoughtco.com/the-wars-of-the-former-yugoslavia-1221861.

Griff Witte, "Ratko Mladic, the 'Butcher of Bosnia,' Guilty of Genocide in Last Balkan War Crimes Trial," *Washington Post,* November 22, 2017, www.washingtonpost.com/world/ratko-mladic-the-butcher-of-bosnia-guilty-of-genocide-in-last-balkan-war-crimes-trial/2017/11/22/8b60f108-cef8-11e7-a87b-47f14b73162a_story.html.

Index

S

Saudi Arabia, 109–114
Schneider, Mark L., 28–31
Serbia, and Bosnian genocide,
10, 33, 34, 59, 75, 87–88
Shaw, Martin, 55–62
Soviet Union, 45, 58, 59
genocide by starvation in
Ukraine, 23–27
Srebrenica massacre, 33, 34,
74, 87–88
Sri Lanka peacekeepers, sexual
abuse by, 91–96
Stalin, Joseph, 23, 24, 59
Sudan/South Sudan, 14, 29,
30, 37–41, 44, 50, 76, 89
Syria, 14, 29, 30, 44, 46, 76

T

Tolbert, David, 68–78
Torres, Alec, 23–27
Trump, Donald, 42, 46, 110,
114
Turkey and Armenian
genocide, 8, 58
denial of Armenian
genocide, 9–10, 16–22,
68–78

U

Ukraine, genocide by
starvation in, 23–27

United Nations, 7, 10, 28, 30,
57
Convention on the
Prevention and
Punishment of the
Crime of Genocide, 7,
10, 12–13, 14, 15, 32, 33,
34, 45, 51, 55, 58, 98, 99
Human Rights Council, 35
peacekeeping efforts, 44–45,
91–96
Security Council, 13, 14, 30,
114
sexual abuse by
peacekeepers, 91–96
United States
complicity in genocide in
Yemen, 109–114
killing of Native Americans
and, 18, 22, 70–71
Office of Global Criminal
Justice, 42–43, 45, 46
prevention of genocide and,
42–46
University of New Hampshire
Tales, 101–103
Uyghurs, 14

V

Vahanian, Noëlle, 16, 21–22
von Joeden-Forgey, Elisa,
47–54

W

X

Y